The Lords Baltimore

Fatti Maschi : Parole Femine

Nan Hayden Agle
and Frances Atchinson Bacon

THE

LORDS BALTIMORE

ILLUSTRATED BY LEONARD VOSBURGH

HOLT, RINEHART AND WINSTON · NEW YORK

Library of Congress Catalog Card Number: 62-10617

90187-0212
Printed in the United States of America

For Ann, Jane, Kimberly, Elizabeth,
Thomas, Richard and William

We wish to thank the following: The Enoch Pratt Free Library, especially the staff of the Maryland Room and Margaret Edwards; the Maryland Historical Society and Eugenia Holland; Mr. Wilbur H. Hunter, Jr., of the Peale Museum; Mr. Robert A. Nicolls of Friends School, Baltimore, for their help with this book; and our understanding and very patient husbands, John N. Agle and Hilary E. Bacon.

NAN HAYDEN AGLE

FRANCES ATCHINSON BACON

Baltimore, Maryland

Contents

The Lords Baltimore

I

Young George Calvert

IT WAS A BITTER February morning, before dawn, in the year 1587 in England. George Calvert, seven years old, was awakened by a tapping noise. At first he thought it was the sleet, beating against the small, leaded panes of his dormer window. He listened, and heard the sound again, clearly. Someone was knocking on the front door. Then followed running footsteps and shrill voices, but he could not make out what was said. George burrowed down in the cozy warmth of his feather bed and pulled the covers over his head. Listen, his mother was crying! Quickly he jumped out of bed.

Shivering with excitement and cold, he pulled on his long, green hose, his full, striped breeches, and struggled into his red doublet, not stopping to put the ruff around his neck. He thrust his feet into woolen house slippers and ran out of his room and down the stairs. As he ran, the great oaken door slammed and he heard horses galloping off. What could be the trouble, so early in the morning?

George stopped, listened, then walked to the door of the winter parlor and looked in. There was his mother, kneeling on her prayer stool by the window. Alicia Calvert was a devout Catholic and no one, not even her son George, dared disturb her at prayers. He tiptoed over to the open fire and held out his hands to warm at the crackling flames. Gay shadows danced on the carved ceiling and on the oak-paneled walls. Quiet as he was, his mother heard him and turned.

She rose, her full skirts billowing around her.

"What is it, Mother? Who came? Why are you crying?"

Alicia Calvert sat in her lady chair near the fire, and George pulled up a fat hassock to sit close at her feet.

"A messenger has brought dreadful news. Your father has gone with him to tell the townsfolk."

"What news, Mother?"

"Mary, Queen of Scots, has been beheaded!"

"Beheaded? You mean somebody cut off her head on purpose?" asked the boy, jumping to his feet. When his mother nodded, he went on, "Poor Queen. I'm glad it wasn't our Queen Elizabeth, aren't you, Mother?"

After a long pause, Alicia Calvert said, "It was Her Majesty who gave the order for the execution. A dreadful thing, and Queen Mary her own blood cousin."

"But why, Mother? Why did she do it?" asked George.

Alicia thought for a moment, then spoke slowly, choosing words a puzzled child could understand.

"Mary, Queen of Scots, was a Catholic when most of her subjects were Protestant. In time, her nobles rose up against her and took her prisoner. Mary managed to escape to England, thinking that her cousin, Queen Elizabeth, would protect her. Mary was wrong. Queen Elizabeth promptly sent her to prison where she stayed for years. Now poor Mary is dead."

"Even if Queen Mary was a Catholic, our Queen didn't have to be so cruel," George argued.

"Fear made Queen Elizabeth cruel. There was a plot to put Mary on the throne and the Queen knew that the only way to save her own head was to take Mary's."

George hugged his mother. "You are a Catholic, don't let them cut off your head."

Alicia smiled. "I'm not a queen, just the wife of Leonard Calvert, a country gentleman of Kiplin, Yorkshire. Like as not my head is safe, though lesser people have lost their lives for their faith."

"I'm glad Father and I are Protestants. I'm glad we go to the Church of England, the Queen's church. I wish you were a Protestant, too, Mother, but I love you, anyway."

Soon, everybody in England had heard the sad story of Mary, Queen of Scots. From the beggars on the streets to the nobles in the castles, everyone was talking of her tragic death.

George and his younger brother, Christopher, and their friend, Toby Matthews, son of the Bishop of Durham, talked about it, too. The Calvert boys visited

Durham regularly; they were being tutored there. After lessons, they would go into the great Durham Cathedral and stand by the door with feet wide apart, craning their necks to see the top of the arches that seemed to reach to heaven in the mysterious shadows far above. In the Galilee Chapel they chased each other around the graceful

pillars or played hide-and-seek. It was quiet and rather scary. Once the verger, in his long black cloak, caught them.

"Come out from behind the Venerable Bede's tomb, you young rapscallions," he ordered in a deep voice.

When the boys came out, shamefaced, he shook his head. "So it's you, Master Toby, and Master George. Haven't you any respect for the dead?" Then, motioning to the tomb, "and him restin' there quiet for four hundred years and more."

Once outside, there was plenty to do, for Durham Cathedral, half fortress, half church, stood on a rocky peninsula, jutting into the River Weare. The boys liked to climb up on top of the thick wall surrounding the Cathedral Close and march around, pretending that they were English soldiers looking for Scots. If there was no sign of the enemy, they would scramble down the steep bank, make twig boats with leaf sails and launch them on the river. Swiftly, the current spun the little boats about and soon they were sailing out of sight around the bend.

Both boys planned to be great naval heroes like their idol, Sir Francis Drake, the sea dog who raided the Spanish ports and captured Spanish treasure ships in the New World. When they were men, they would defend England from all of her enemies, especially Spain. There were rumors going around now that the Catholic King Philip II of Spain was building an armada to sweep down on England, punish the Protestants, get rid of the sea raiders, and let everyone know that Spain was the greatest power in the world.

Time proved that these rumors were true. In May of 1588, when George Calvert was eight years old, the Great Armada—one hundred and thirty-two ships, galleons, men-of-war, and smaller vessels, loaded with guns, infantry, and supplies—sailed from Lisbon for England, reaching Plymouth in July.

To warn the people that the enemy was coming, signal fires were lighted on every castle rampart from Land's End to the Border.

"To arms, Englishmen!"

All of England, Protestants and Catholics alike, rallied behind Queen Elizabeth against the Spanish.

It was a dreadful fight. Many of the Spanish ships were wrecked on the rocky coast of Scotland. Some Spaniards landed in Ireland, hoping to find water for the crews, and there they were attacked by the Irish. Sixty-three Spanish ships were lost, but not one English ship.

When at last the fighting was over, bells in every church in England rang out, singing of victory. The Cathedral of Durham was filled with people, giving thanks to God.

At Kiplin, Leonard Calvert, George's father, left his large flocks of sheep with able shepherds while he took George and Toby, who was visiting, to show them a Spanish galleon wrecked on the beach. The boys had wanted to go to Scotland, where much of the fleet had been wrecked, but it was too far. But then news came of

a ship wrecked off the Yorkshire coast, a two-day ride across the wild moors. When, at last, the boys stood on a high cliff looking down at the huge ship, on its side like a beached whale, George said, "How could we win, Father? That ship is much larger than any of ours."

"Too large," replied Leonard Calvert. "Our smaller ships, newer in design, can sail upwind. Our guns have longer range. Our good English sailors know the water and every reef and rock on our coast. With Lord Howard commanding the fleet, and Drake and Hawkins fighting with him, how could we lose?"

Toby boasted, "My father says God had a hand in the victory. He says God sent the storm and the fog to confuse the enemy."

"Aye, your father, the Bishop, is right about that. And don't forget another reason the Spanish lost the fight; they had paid soldiers who fought for money, while our men were fighting for England."

As they mounted their horses for the long ride home, George's father added, "It's a grand thing to be an Englishman!"

2

George Calvert, First Lord Baltimore

THE DURHAM COACH, drawn by six horses, rolled into the town of Oxford and stopped at the Mitre Inn. The coach door swung open and a slim, dark-eyed youth stepped down.

A servant came forward.

"Master George Calvert from Kiplin?" he asked.

"Yes," George replied.

"I was sent to fetch you and your luggage to Trinity College."

George was glad to see the man, for his bones ached from the long, rough trip—three days over rutted roads, and two nights spent in strange, noisy inns. He was gladder still to enter the gate of Trinity College and finally climb the stone steps to his room. He threw open the casement windows and looked down to the quadrangle below, where groups of students were talking together. So many new people to meet; George wondered which ones would be his friends. He scarcely had time to change his dusty doublet and hose before the dinner gong sounded and he joined the other students at the long refectory table in the Great Hall. From that moment on, the days flew by, every minute full.

George studied grammar, logic, rhetoric, arithmetic, geometry, astronomy, music, and, of course, Latin, French, and Spanish. After classes he learned about England and the world of 1594.

Many a night the candles burned short while the boys talked of the heroes of the time: Sir Walter Raleigh, the gallant explorer, poet, and courtier; Drake and his fabled ship, *Golden Hind;* Will Shakespeare, the popular playwright. Some of the boldest students even broke college rules to slip off and see a play of his when the traveling company came near Oxford Town.

Everybody was reading and talking about the New World. What a fabulous place it must be! Some said grapes there were as big as peaches. And gold was free for anyone to put in his pocket. In England, most of the gold dropped into Queen Elizabeth's velvet purse.

Late one night, two students were in George's room arguing about the Queen and her court, a favorite subject. George said hotly, "This much I do know, the Queen hath no right to tell her subjects how they shall worship God."

"Softly. If those rash words of yours ever reach the royal ear you will feel the bite of an ax on your neck," warned Dick, a friend from Sussex. "And pray, why be so concerned? You and I and all other sensible people in England are Protestants, like our Sovereign."

George answered quickly, "My mother is a Roman Catholic. She dares defy the Queen's orders."

William, a red-haired boy, lounging in the window seat, shrugged his shoulders. "Your mother is a brave woman or else a foolish one." He leaned forward and whispered, "My lackey brought news from the street that three Catholics were executed last night. A rumor, perhaps."

"It is no rumor," George told them. "It's the dreadful truth. I, for one, think the Queen had no right to order a man's death just because of his belief."

"Treason, treason!" laughed William and tossed a cushion at George.

"I agree with George." Dick defended his friend. "The people should have some rights. Isn't it the job of Parliament to speak for the people?"

There was no end to the argument. It went on and on until at last the boys headed sleepily for their rooms.

When George was alone, he sat for some time thinking, elbows on his desk, chin cupped in his hands. His mind was racing with new ideas, and he could not sleep. He thought, maybe in the New World a man will be able to speak and worship as he pleases. He began to picture this land, far on the other side of the ocean. In time he would go there himself, but first he would need to make his fortune. He could work with his father as a grazier. Leonard Calvert was a prosperous man, with thousands of sheep, which meant both mutton and wool, gold in the purse, and an Oxford education for his son.

Being a grazier was all right, George thought, but he really wished he could be a courtier like Sir Walter Raleigh. It would take more than a wish for a commoner to get a start at court, however. What he needed was an influential friend to speak for him.

When George had finished his studies at Oxford, in 1597, he, like all young men whose parents could afford it, set out on a tour of the Continent. Aside from the pleasure of seeing new sights and meeting new people, the trip would make him a man of the world. But first young Calvert wanted to see London and, in high spirits, he traveled by barge on the Thames to London Town.

He took lodgings as near as possible to the famous Mermaid Tavern, in the hope of seeing Will Shakespeare or Ben Jonson. All day long he strolled about the town, visiting Cheapside, St. Paul's Cathedral, and the Tower of London, where so many famous people had been impris-

oned or had even lost their lives. Late in the afternoon, he returned to the tavern, so excited by the many new sights that he barely tasted his lamb pie. Tomorrow, he decided, he would see one of Shakespeare's plays, for no college rules bound him now.

Early the next afternoon he crossed London Bridge and, taking long steps, headed for The Theatre. The shops that lined both sides of the bridge tempted him to buy, but he did not stop. A white flag atop the peaked roof of the theater told him that a comedy was playing that day. Good, he was in a holiday mood. He dropped sixpence in the box at the door for a choice seat in the balcony.

"Prithee tell me, what is the play?" he asked.

" 'The Taming of the Shrew,' sir, and a romping piece it is," answered a member of the troupe who was collecting the money.

George was glad to be early. It gave him time to buy an orange from a hawker and eat it, being careful not to drop any juice on his new, plum-colored doublet. It was a bright day. He leaned over and looked down into the courtyard, where the gay clothes of the audience made a brave sight, indeed. Just before the play started, three gallants, dressed in the latest fashion, came in and, with great to-do, took their places in the balcony by the left side of the stage, amid a bowing and scraping from the common folk.

A roll of drums announced the beginning of the play. From the moment the first player stepped onto the stage,

George was spellbound by the magic of Shakespeare's words. The comedy was over all too soon. Then, as was the custom, clowns came forward to do tricks. George threw them a penny when they had finished. A bear fight was to follow, but he did not wait. He wanted to be off the streets, safe in his lodgings, before dark. It would be a shame to lose his full purse to a robber with the Continent waiting for him just across the English Channel.

George would never forget gay Paris, the ruins of ancient Rome, or the beauty of the Rhine River in Germany. The people were even more interesting than the places. The most interesting of all was a small, hunchbacked man, Sir Robert Cecil, whom George met at the

English Embassy in Paris. The older man liked George at once and came to appreciate his strong character and promise of ability. Cecil, who was Secretary of State, was in a position to start George on a political career, which he did when they both returned to England.

Like most young men of the seventeenth century, or any other, George Calvert did not keep all his thoughts on his work. He found time to woo Anne Mynne, the lovely daughter of John Mynne, a gentleman of Hertfordshire. Anne found her suitor so attractive, with his pointed beard and brown, sparkling eyes that in 1603 she married him. They made their home in London.

The year 1603 was an important one for England as well as for George Calvert. Queen Elizabeth died, and James VI of Scotland, son of Mary, Queen of Scots, became James I of England. Although he sat on Elizabeth's throne, he was never the strong and wise ruler she had been.

The following year, Sir Robert Cecil made Calvert his private secretary. This was an important position, for Cecil was second only to the King in England. To honor their patron, George and Anne named their first child— a son—Cecil.

On a cold March morning, the proud parents and assembled company trouped into the little church at Bexley, Kent, not far from London. No one was happier than Anne as she looked down at the tiny baby, his pink face almost lost in his large christening cap. The voluminous skirts of the christening gown were trimmed in *point devisé* lace. Baby Cecil Calvert had three illustrious godparents: Sir Robert Cecil, the Earl of Cumberland, and Lady Wotton.

In 1605, King James I paid a royal visit to Oxford. Both townsfolk and University people outdid themselves to provide a fitting welcome for the noble company. Silken banners waved, and tapestries hung from upper windows. Everybody was in holiday dress, marching out to welcome the King and his courtiers.

There was jostling and shoving as the crowd tried to catch a glimpse of the royal visitors. King James was resplendent in purple velvet, his cloak lined in ermine, his noble horse decked out in the royal trappings. Queen Anne rode beside him, her fair hair and crimson brocaded gown covered with a hooded cloak of blue. After the royal couple, came the lords and ladies of the court. Riding together near the end of the cavalcade were Sir Robert Cecil, now the Earl of Salisbury, and his secretary, George Calvert.

Then followed sumptuous banquets: boar's head with apples, roasted peacocks in tender pastries, great platters of fruit, of which King James was very fond, and the sweet wines which he liked all too well. The servants rushed to and fro, filling the flagons as fast as they were emptied. Then came the speeches in Latin, of course, and long. King James nodded approvingly at each flowery phrase. Lute players and singers entertained the company with "Who is Sylvia?," Will Shakespeare's lovely song.

Last of all, Master's degrees from Oxford were awarded to many distinguished men: the Duke of Lennox; the Earls of Oxford, Northumberland, and Salisbury; and one commoner, George Calvert.

One sunny morning, not long after the visit to Oxford, George Calvert was at Court with the Earl of Salisbury. The King, after a good breakfast, twice looked down his long nose at the young man; then his mood changed and he actually smiled at George. In fact, he was impressed enough with Calvert to send him to Ireland several times on official business. On these trips, George did his work so well that King James retained him after Cecil's death in 1612. In 1617, His Majesty knighted Calvert as a reward for distinguished service.

George, pleased as a gamecock with his title, hurried home to his family, a large one by now. While his good wife, Anne, and the older children bowed and addressed him as "Sir George" in fun, he stroked his pointed beard with pride. He took the baby, Grace, from her mother and tossed her high. Elizabeth, the next oldest, hugged her father around the knees saying, "Papa, Papa," another title which pleased Sir George Calvert. The children played at being knights and kings and queens. Cecil, the oldest, pretending to be king, knighted his younger brothers, saying, "Rise, Sir Phillip and Sir Leonard."

In time, King James made Calvert Secretary of State and a member of his important Privy Council. Sir George accepted these responsible positions with misgivings, modest man that he was, for he felt that he would never be the statesman Sir Robert Cecil had been. George had many other things on his mind. By this time he had been given land in County Longford, Ireland, by King James, as a mark of royal favor. For years he had been a member of the Virginia Company which had backed Sir Walter Raleigh's settlements in the New World. As one of the counselors in the New England Company, George had dealings with the Plymouth Colony. In 1620, the very year the Mayflower sailed, he had purchased a plantation in New Found Land, far north of Plymouth, and recently the King had given him a charter for the Province of Avalon there.

Besides being interested in far-off lands, he and Anne were planning a new home. It was going to be a fine, big house at Kiplin on the River Swale, big enough to hold ten children and many grandchildren. Surrounding the house were one thousand acres of land for crops and cattle. Already, Inigo Jones, the finest architect in England, was at work on the plans. It would be an up-to-date seventeenth century house, made of brick, with square chimneys instead of the stone towerlike chimneys now going out of fashion.

Alas, before the new house was completed, Anne died, leaving a new baby. George, in deep sorrow, secretly turned to the Roman Catholic religion of his mother, hoping to find comfort. His boyhood friend, Toby, now Sir Toby Matthews, who lived in London, had already become a Catholic convert. This, too, influenced George.

When the King asked Calvert to serve on a committee to try a group of men who refused to belong to the Church of England, George could keep his secret no longer. How could he send men to the gallows or even to prison for being Catholics when he was one himself? He publicly announced his conversion to the Roman Catholic Church, and, on February 12, 1625, resigned as Secretary of State.

This was a blow to Protestant King James. The King, unpredictable as he was, might have chopped off his Secretary's Catholic head. Instead, he accepted Calvert's resignation, and because of the affection he held for this brave man, made him Baron of Baltimore in the Kingdom of Ireland. Thus he became the First Lord Baltimore.

After the death of James I in 1625, Calvert stayed in favor with the new Protestant King, Charles I. Now, at last, a wealthy man with all his duties as a public servant over, George turned his full attention to the New World.

3

The New World

Two YEARS LATER, Lord Baltimore sat in the study of his new home, Kiplin Hall, Yorkshire. On the heavy oak table before him lay manuscripts, letters, and books. One letter he read and reread, glancing from time to time at a map of the New World on the wall. After a while, he rose from his chair, and, still deep in thought, pulled the bell rope for a servant.

"You rang, my lord?"

"Kindly summon my eldest son. I would speak with him."

A few moments later, Cecil, now a young man of twenty-one with a strong, serious face, came into the study.

"You sent for me, Father?"

George Calvert nodded, pulling a chair for Cecil closer to his own. "A letter has just arrived from our province of Avalon and I am not at all pleased with the report."

"What has happened? Earlier news was favorable."

"Too favorable. I was a fool to swallow stories about a colony that told of a mermaid in the harbor."

"A mermaid?" exclaimed Cecil.

"Let me read you what Richard Whitbourne, a sea captain, hath written," said Lord Baltimore, picking up a document.

" 'As I was standing by the waterside in the harbor of St. John's, I espied a strange creature very swiftly swimming toward me, looking cheerfully, as it were a woman. . . . When this strange creature saw that I went from it, it dived a little under water, whereby I beheld the shoulders and back down to the middle, to be as white and smooth as the back of a man, and from the middle to the hinder part, pointing like a broad hooked arrow.' "

Cecil shook his head, "Captain Whitbourne must have been ill of a fever."

George continued, "No, he tells further of this creature trying to climb in a small boat and being clouted over the head by the terrified sailors. But, enough of mermaids. . . ."

Lord Baltimore looked at his son intently and went on, "You are familiar with the Avalon charter. As you recall, we have proprietary rights, giving us absolute power over the land." He thought a moment, then laid his hand on his son's arm and said, "I would see this place with my own eyes, for it is more than a business venture to me, more than a new colony for England. For some time I have been thinking that there should be a place

where a man could live in peace, free to worship God as
a Catholic or a Protestant. I will make Avalon that place,
if it please God."

Cecil nodded. "And I will help you, Father."

Together they studied the map of the New World.
"There, to the south you see Jamestown, Raleigh's settlement in Virginia," George pointed out. "And north,
along the coast, is Plymouth, where the Pilgrims settled.
Still further north lies New Found Land, with Avalon
jutting out into the sea."

Cecil could almost see the New World across the
ocean. "When do we sail, Father?" he asked with excitement.

"This time I cannot take you with me," answered
Lord Baltimore. "While I am away you will be the head

of the family. You will attend to our affairs here and in Ireland."

Cecil's disappointment showed in his face. "Let Leonard stay home and take your place, Father. I'm the oldest son, I should go with you."

"It is because you are the eldest that you are the one to take my place in England." George turned back to his papers and Cecil knew it was useless to argue.

That spring, the spring of 1627, Lord Baltimore sailed for New Found Land. Although he had never crossed the Atlantic before, he had sailed to Spain and France many times. So an ocean voyage and life aboard ship were not new to him. He was anxious to reach Avalon and impatient with the slow passing of the days and weeks. To make time go more quickly he read and reread, "Westward Hoe to Avalon," Whitbourne's glowing report of the province:

"There are many fruites, pears, sour cherries, filberds, and of these berries and fruits the store is so great that the mariners . . . have often gathered at once, more than half a hogshead would hold." George looked up at the white sails and blue sky, then returned to the account, which told of "strawberries red and white, flowers, herbs, penguins big as geese, and nightengales singing softly."

Finally, the ship sailed into Trinity Harbor, New Found Land. George Calvert felt excitement from his boots to the crown of his wide black hat. The New World at last! Great bare rocks towered along the coast, high waves crashing against them. Though midsummer, it was

a cold, gray day. Calvert pulled his cloak around him to keep out the wind. As he stepped into the small boat to go ashore, he thought that no mermaid in her right mind would spend any time in this harbor.

The weather-beaten settlers who greeted him were a sorry looking lot. That night, over a dinner of fish chowder, fried herring, and fillet of cod, the men had only troubles to report to Lord Baltimore.

"The summer is too short, m'Lord," said one. "It is late in the spring before you can break ground for seed, and the killing frost comes early."

Another added, "A root can hardly take hold on what little soil there is between the boulders."

George nodded, savoring a tasty fillet, browned to the King's taste. "The fish seem plentiful."

Everybody agreed to that. A settler with a heavy beard said, "Fishing is our one good industry, m'Lord, and our daily food. Without the cod, the people of Avalon would have perished long ago." He sipped his ale and went on, "After September, the only green thing around here is hope and very little of that will last out the winter."

Lord Baltimore was an obstinate Englishman. Cold weather and rocky soil would never defeat him, so he thought. To prove how sure he was that the colony would succeed, he told the men to build granaries and store-houses, as well as a large residence for himself and his family.

After a short stay, he went back to England for the

winter, determined to return to Avalon the following
spring with his children and his second wife, Joan. He
would live there himself. That would show those chicken-
livered colonists there was more in Avalon than hope!

When George told Joan his plans for settling in
Avalon, she was very fearful. She was young, and the
responsibilities of marriage to an older man with so many
children took all her courage, even in familiar surround-
ings. The thought of leaving England and her own family
and friends saddened her; and the task of taking the
younger children to a strange, wild land terrified her.
Nevertheless, she knew she must go with her husband to
the New World. So she kept her fears to herself and
began to make plans for the trip: ordering warm clothes
and boots for the children, making lists of food and medicines, and collecting school books.

From the King, Lord Baltimore bought a stout ship
of four hundred tons. She was named the *Ark,* and George
thought to himself that she really would be the Ark when
his wife, his children, and forty able colonists came
aboard.

Cecil again stayed in England to take his father's
place. This time, however, he did not mind being left
behind because the beautiful Lady Anne Arundel had
just become his bride. She was the fourth daughter of
Lord Thomas Arundel, a Catholic. Cecil, like all of Lord
Baltimore's children, had become a Catholic, too. As the
Ark sailed, and Lord and Lady Baltimore waved good-by
to Cecil and his bride, how Joan wished she could change

places with Lady Anne, and stay at home in dear England.

After six weeks of keeping the young Calverts from plunging overboard or falling from the rigging, Joan was as eager to come into Trinity Harbor as her husband. Fearful as she was of the New World, at least it would be dry land.

George found that the settlers had built the storehouses that he had ordered. His new house, made of stone, was large and impressive. The children ran from room to room, laughing and talking together about who would sleep where.

George Calvert scarcely had time to sit down at his desk in his new study facing the sea before one of the settlers rushed in, shouting, "M'Lord, m'Lord, French ships are in the harbor! Already they've captured two of our vessels. We have no warships and no fort. What shall we do?"

"We have Englishmen," Lord Baltimore said proudly. "Send out the *Ark* and the *Dove*. Man the guns and let us show those pirates that Englishmen are fighting men."

The *Ark,* with the *Dove,* a ship that had recently arrived from England, quickly captured the enemy and recaptured their own two ships. Sixty-seven prisoners were seized. George Calvert found that it was an expensive victory, for all the prisoners were hungry, and there was little enough for the colonists to eat. All prisoners belonged to the King and would be sent to England, but meanwhile they had to be fed.

As Lord Baltimore well knew, the trouble between France and England had begun soon after Charles I came to the throne. The King's favorite nobleman, the Duke of Buckingham, had brought him a royal bride from

France. She was Henrietta Maria, the fifteen-year-old sister of the King of France, and a Catholic. Before the marriage, Buckingham had promised to help the English Catholics, a promise which was soon forgotten, and war between France and England followed. Lord Baltimore little thought that any part of this war would reach him across the ocean. Now he felt uneasy, even in victory, for he knew that no Englishman was allowed to take up arms without written permission. He wrote to the Duke of Buckingham: "I came to build and settle and sow; and I am fallen to fighting Frenchmen."

Calling his son Leonard, now a young man, to him, he said, "Here is a letter to the Duke of Buckingham, telling him of our naval battle. Sail at once and deliver it at Court. A ship will be leaving at high tide, taking a cargo of salt codfish back to England."

When Leonard reached England, he found that Buckingham had been assassinated by one of his own officers, so he personally delivered the letter to the King. King Charles readily gave his approval to the naval battle and granted Lord Baltimore the right to the prize money for the captured ships. Leonard thanked him and returned to Avalon on the *St. Claude,* which His Majesty lent to Lord Baltimore for a year, an extra reward for his victory.

George Calvert had conquered the French, but he found he could not conquer the winter in New Found Land. Bitter winds blew constantly from the sea. The ground was frozen hard, and ice covered the rocks like sugar frosting. Even the strongest settlers became sick from a diet of salt fish and little else.

When Lord Baltimore's own children began to cough and shiver with fever and chills, he became alarmed and said to his wife, "You must leave Avalon at once. I will make arrangements for you to take the children to Jamestown, in Virginia, where the climate is warm."

"Not without you," Joan protested.

Lord Baltimore was firm. "I must stay here with the colony or give it up altogether. You will be safe in Jamestown. My friend, John Harvey, the Governor of Virginia, will make you welcome and see that you and the children are comfortable and protected. Several of your friends from England are there and will keep you company. As soon as spring comes I will send for you."

Lady Baltimore stood for a long time without a word. Then she raised her chin high and said, "You know what is best for us, my lord."

She packed hurriedly. Now and then, when no one was looking, she wept into her handkerchief of fine linen, edged with handmade lace. Her mother had given it to her, and thinking of her mother far away in England, she wept again. A few days later, she and the children bade Lord Baltimore farewell and sailed for Jamestown.

George Calvert missed his family, although many times during the long, severe winter he thanked God that they were not at Avalon with him. The weather was so bitterly cold and there was so much sickness that George knew he was fortunate to be alive when spring finally returned. He also knew he would have to give up his plans for Avalon. It was hard to admit defeat.

Discouraged, he wrote to his King:

Avalon, August 19, 1629.
Most gracious and dread Sovreign:
    Your Majesty may please to understand . . . that from the middlest of October to the middlest of May there is a sad face of winter upon all this land. . . . My house hath been a hospital all this winter; of a hundred persons, fifty sick at a time, myself being one. I am determined to commit this place to fishermen that are better able to encounter storms and hard weather, and to remove myself with some forty persons to your Majesty's dominion, Virginia; where, if your Majesty will please to grant me a precinct of land, with such privileges as the King, your father . . . was pleased to grant me here, I shall endeavor, to the utmost of my power, to deserve it and pray for your Majesty's long and happy reign.
Your Majesty's most humble and faithful servant,
                            George Baltimore

By slow ship, George's letter traveled to King Charles I, and by slow ship, His Majesty's reply, bearing the royal seal, came back to Avalon.

    "Right Trustie, and well-beloved, We greet you well:
    "Seeing that your plantation in New Found Land . . . hath not answered your expectation,

we, out of our princely care for you, hath thought
fit to advise you . . . to return to your native
country."

If George Calvert had received this royal command,
he would have been obliged to return to England at once,
but it so happened that by the time the letter reached
Avalon, he was on his way to Virginia.

During the winter, Jamestown had been good to
Lord Baltimore's family. Lady Baltimore had enjoyed the
social life of the colony and the children had played and
studied their lessons with the children of Jamestown.
When Lord Baltimore arrived, his family greeted him
with joy. However, Governor Harvey of Virginia gave
him a cool, formal, "I bid you good day, your lordship."

Lord Baltimore did not understand this coolness of
his old friend, whom he had known in England, until the
local news reached his ear. It seemed that Jamestown had
lost its charter with the Virginia Company of London because the colonists wanted to be self-governing, and the
Crown objected. The Governor, knowing that Lord Baltimore was anxious to found a colony in the south, was
afraid that King Charles might hand over the Virginia
settlement to him. Because Virginians feared that Catholic Spain might try to take over their colony, they feared
Catholic noblemen, particularly Lord Baltimore. Determined to force him to leave Jamestown as soon as possible,
the Governor demanded that Calvert take the oath of
supremacy, which put the state before the church, knowing perfectly well that Catholics were forbidden to do so.

When Lord Baltimore refused, the Governor sent a petition to the King, asking him to order Calvert home.

The Governor was not the only one at Jamestown anxious to see the last of Lord Baltimore. Captain William Claibourne, Secretary for the colony of Virginia, ran a trading post at Kent Island, which lay in the northern end of the Chesapeake Bay about 175 miles from Jamestown. Claibourne was making a fortune there trading furs with the Indians and he had no intention of letting anyone take Kent Island from him. In fact, he did not even want George Calvert to look at it.

George had no wish to take anything from anybody. However, he did not want to return to England until he had found a place for his colony. He ignored the unfriendly attitude and for weeks he explored the country looking for the right place to settle.

After a trip to the land lying south of the Virginia colony, he said to his wife, "Although the climate there is warm and the ground fertile, the river anchorage is not deep enough for English trading ships."

At dawn, a few days later, Lord Baltimore again went exploring. With a guide and two youths he left Jamestown harbor in an English shallop, a light boat with oars and sails, the first one of its kind ever built in the New World. They headed north. When the shallop entered the wide mouth of the Chesapeake Bay, George Calvert exclaimed, "Never before have I seen such a beautiful body of water!"

"It's twelve miles across, m'Lord," the guide told him.

They sailed on. A fish jumped out of the water and flopped back. Far off came the cry of a loon. Green forests lined the banks of the Bay—great hickory trees, oak, and cypress, tall enough to make a ship's mast—with blue sky above and blue-green water all around. "Beautiful, beautiful," Calvert said again and again. In his heart he knew he had found the place for his colony.

Late into the night, George Calvert talked with his wife. "I must go to England and speak with King Charles face to face. I cannot trust a letter to bear my news. I must tell him, myself, about this place and beg him to give me a grant for it right away. I will sail on the next ship and return for you, please God, as soon as the grant for our land is in my hand, signed by His Majesty and sealed with the Great Seal of England."

Lord Baltimore left his wife and children in Jamestown, under the protection of the Governor, and returned to England. He soon had an audience with the King, who thought that Calvert looked tired and thin, and who urged this dedicated man to give up further plans for a colony and to stay in England where he could take better care of his health.

Lord Baltimore would not be turned from his purpose. Again and again he begged the King to give him a grant for his colony. George found, however, that changing the mind of a king takes time. He became anxious to see his family, yet he could not leave England without the grant. He sent a letter to the Governor of Virginia, telling him that the ship *St. Claude* would arrive shortly to bring Lady Baltimore and the children home.

The *St. Claude* made the voyage to Virginia safely, but on the return trip it was wrecked off the coast of England. There were no survivors. George Calvert, deeply shaken when the tragic news reached him, wrote to a friend, who had recently lost his own wife, calling himself a man of sorrows. "All things in the world pass away," he wrote, "wife, children, honor, wealth, friends and what else is dear to flesh and blood. They are but lent us till God pleases to call them back again."

Lord Baltimore now renewed his efforts to get the grant for his colony. After a time His Majesty offered George land south of the Jamestown Colony, but this was not what he wanted. The Chesapeake Bay region was so perfect that he would settle for nothing else. At last the King gave him what he wanted. The grant read:

> All lands lying north of Virginia, on both sides of the Chesapeake Bay, and including the whole peninsula of the Eastern Shore. On the Western Shore, the grant is to extend from the 40th degree North Latitude, which is the southern boundary of New England, to the mouth of the Potomac River.

In return for his charter, Lord Baltimore was to pay to the King, "One fifth part of any gold and silver mined in the colony." He was to swear allegiance to the Crown, and to pay an annual rent to the King at Windsor Castle of two Indian arrowheads on Whitsuntide. Charles I directed that there would be no taxing between England and America and that "the laws governing the colony would be agreeable to reason and to the laws of England."

Lord Baltimore wrote the charter for his new colony himself, leaving a blank space for its name.

King Charles read the document and said, "Let us give it a name in honor of the Queen, Henrietta Maria. What think you of Mary Land?"

"Mary Land," George repeated. "Methinks it hath a noble sound. Mary Land it shall be." Taking the charter from the hand of his King, he filled in the blank, writing boldly, for the first time, "MARYLAND."

George Calvert began at once to work on the plans for establishing the colony of Maryland. First, he must interest the right people all over England in this venture. With the help of a young Jesuit priest, Father White, he wrote a pamphlet describing his colony, which was to be founded on religious freedom, where there would not only be a good life, but also a prosperous one, for those bold enough to take the risk.

Suddenly, on the fifteenth of April, 1632, George Calvert, First Lord Baltimore, died. He left to his son, Cecil, the title, Baron of Baltimore, and the responsibility of founding the colony of Maryland.

4

The Voyage

WARDOUR CASTLE, home of the Arundel family at Tisbury in Wiltshire, was bursting with activity. There was so much coming and going that Lord Arundel, father-in-law of Cecil Calvert, the new Lord Baltimore, went out into the rose garden to be alone for a time. Here his daughter, Anne, found him.

"Father, what troubles you?"

"Ever since the charter of Maryland passed the Great Seal, this whole place has been humming like a beehive. From morning till night the great hall is crowded with gentlemen with full purses, anxious to sign for the voyage. In the kitchen, the cooks forget to baste the fowls on the spit for listening to the indentured servants bragging that they will soon be landowners."

Anne laughed. "You are just as eager to go to the New World as Jed, the drummer boy, Father. As for my husband, he counts the days until the sailing."

Inside the castle, Cecil Calvert, the Second Lord Baltimore, Proprietary of the colony of Maryland, stood at the window of the library, looking across the wide lawn. Then he turned back to the papers spread out on a massive oak table. Since his father's death, he felt as though he were the king of a small kingdom. To him and his descendants forever, had been given the ownership of Maryland, and the power to make laws, levy taxes, confer titles, build towns, make war and peace, and coin money. This was a heavy responsibility for a young man of twenty-seven.

There was a knock at the door and in walked his brothers, Leonard, Phillip, and George. Leonard and George were going with the colonists; Phillip planned to follow later. With them were five other gentlemen: Thomas Cornwallis, Esq.; Jerome Hawley, Esq.; Thomas Greene; and Frederick and Edward Wintour. Cornwallis and Hawley were the Commissioners appointed to help the Governor with the affairs of the colony.

Cornwallis bowed and said, "M'Lord, we come to leave with you our monies for the expedition. I am taking ten men. Here is two hundred pounds sterling, twenty for each man for transportation. Now, pray tell me what lands will I get for this outlay of mine?"

Lord Baltimore was a patient man. He passed his hand wearily over his eyes. "Methinks I can rattle these terms off in my sleep. If you take five men you get one thousand acres of good Maryland land; less than five, one hundred acres for each man. So with ten men you will be entitled to two thousand acres. Is that clear?"

Young Frederick Wintour spoke up, "That answers

my question, for I am taking three men. The carpenter from our village, his wife, and three sons want to go. What of them?"

Cecil replied, "One hundred acres will be granted to this man, one hundred to his wife, and fifty to each child over sixteen. Fifty acres will be given indentured servants after they have worked seven years. This will pay for their passage and give them their freedom."

Then he added, "The tax to the Proprietary is twelve pence a year for each fifty acres of land."

Leonard warned, "Remember that everyone must take apparel, bedding, arms, tools, and seed for one whole year. We want no starving colonists in Maryland, as they had in Plymouth and Virginia."

Lord Baltimore went over these instructions many times during the following months. Finally, two hundred people were signed on for the voyage. Among the two hundred were seventeen gentlemen adventurers, a number of skilled carpenters, wainwrights, shipbuilders, brickmakers, farmers, one man who could "clave, lath and pale," and a few brave women, wives, and indentured servants. Mistress Margaret Brent, long a friend of the Calverts, sent five servants, so that land would be set aside for her and others of her family, who planned to come to the colony a little later.

Each colonist was told to take two hats, two suits, three pairs of stockings, shoes, one ax, one saw, one shovel, nails, one grindstone, one spit, one gridiron, a pot, a kettle, a frying pan, and seven ells of canvas for a bed and bolster, to be filled with corn husks in Maryland.

Besides this long list, a man needed "a musket, ten pounds of powder, ten pounds of lead, bullets and goose shot; also a sword, a belt, a bandolier and a flask." The colonists knew they could not depend solely on the seventeen gentlemen adventurers for protection.

Cecil Calvert was so busy he failed to realize that he and his colony had powerful enemies both in England and in Virginia. Representatives of Virginia in England, afraid of the Catholics, and afraid of losing both land and settlers to the Maryland colony, did everything possible to prevent the *Ark* and the *Dove* from sailing. They spread false rumors that, under the new Proprietary, only Catholics would be allowed in Maryland. They circulated petitions against Cecil and even wrote letters of protest to the King. Although Cecil held meetings to explain his plans and made promises under oath that all faiths would be welcome in his colony, he was not able to settle this argument with the Virginia colony. At last he realized that he would have to stay in England while Maryland's charter was under attack. He was bitterly disappointed.

Cecil thought of his father, the First Lord Baltimore, and how he had planned this colony to be a place where men could worship God in freedom. Although most of the leaders were Catholics, many of the prospective colonists were Protestants. How could he establish the first colony with freedom of religion in the New World if he did not go there? Yet, if he did not stay in England to take care of the colony's interests, he might lose Maryland. He resolved to join the colonists as soon as he could settle the vexing problems. Perhaps it would not take long. In the meantime, the colony would be in good hands with his brother Leonard as Governor, and Father White, a scholar and Jesuit missionary, as spiritual leader.

Lord Baltimore thoughtfully composed a letter of instruction to guide the colonists.

> His Lordship requires his said Governor and Commissioners that in their voyage to Mary Land they be very careful to preserve unity and peace amongst all the passengers on Shipp-board . . . and treate the Protestants with as much mildness and favor as Justice will permit. And this to be observed at Land as well as at Sea.

As soon as they landed in Maryland, the colonists were to build a fort and a church, plant crops, and establish friendly relations with the natives.

Delays and more delays! Twice the sailing was postponed. At last, on November 22, 1633, the *Ark* and the *Dove* were loaded and ready in the harbor at Cowes. On shipboard were barrels of dried fish, tuns of small beer, casks of claret wine, cheeses and flour, tools and all the provisions the colonists needed to take care of themselves until the first crops were in.

Leonard Calvert and Father White stood at the rail of the *Ark,* the master ship. She weighed about four hundred tons and was "cod-head and mackerel tail, and high out of the water." They watched a gentle east wind fill

the sails of the *Dove,* the sistership, a fifty-ton pinnace. As soon as the small ship had cleared the harbor, the *Ark* weighed anchor and followed. A cheer went up from the friends and families on shore.

Father White raised his hand to bless them.

"I need your blessing, too, Father," said Leonard. "For the first time I feel the weight of this venture upon me. Always before my father and oldest brother have spoken the last word."

Father White turned and looked at the handsome young man beside him. With his black eyes, pointed beard, coat of fine cloth, and wide-brimmed hat with its plume, Leonard Calvert was the very picture of a cavalier.

"It is God who always has the last word," replied Father White. "With His help, this venture will succeed."

England and the Isle of Wight were scarcely out of sight when the *Dragon*, a merchantman of six hundred tons, came alongside the *Ark* and proposed a race. For an hour, the two ships tried to outstrip each other. It was great sport for everyone aboard. Trumpets blared and the crews and passengers shouted encouragement. Although the *Ark* was lighter and carried one less sail, she held her own and might have won the race if her captain had not given orders to drop back. He had realized that the *Dove* was being left far behind, and he did not want to lose sight of her.

When the *Dove* caught up, her captain warned that two lights would be hung on the masthead if ever she was in trouble. And she was that same night! A strong wind came up and the sea rolled and tossed, driving both ships off their course.

On the *Ark,* the lookout in the crow's-nest shouted, "Distress lights on the *Dove* to starboard!"

The *Ark* did her best to reach the little ship, but it was all she could do to keep herself afloat. When the wind died down at dawn, there was no sign of the *Dove.* All day the passengers on the *Ark* kept their eyes on the horizon, hoping to see the sistership.

Although Father White thought the pinnace had sunk, he said, "There is always hope." His prayers comforted the anxious passengers.

Several days later, the captain of the *Ark* saw a sunfish swimming toward the sun. He shook his head. "It's a sure sign a storm is coming."

Sure enough, that very night, such a storm came upon them that all feared the *Ark* would join the *Dove* at the bottom of the sea.

Father White wrote this account of it.

About 10 o'clock at night a dark cloud poured forth a violent shower. And such a furious hurricane followed close upon it, that it was necessary to run with all speed to take in sail: and this could not be done quickly enough to prevent the mainsail, the only one we were carrying, from being split from top to toae, and one part cast into the sea. This amazed the stoutest hearts, even of the sailors. The ship, without sail or rudder, drifted about like a dish in the water. We were in feare of imminent death all this night, never looking to see day in this world, till at length it pleased God to send some

ease, and by little and little still more, we were
with milder weather freed from all these horrours.

The sea stayed angry for another day, rolling the
ship and rattling the pewter plates and tankards in the
galley.

On deck, Leonard Calvert and the captain were talking as they enjoyed the sunshine once again.

"I feel in my bones that we will have a sweet passage
from now on," the captain said. "With our course set due
west we should reach the New World in six weeks or
less."

"My wish is to go south and stop at the Fortunate
Islands off the coast of Africa, to pick up salt and seed,"
replied Leonard. "My brother hath made a great outlay
of money for this expedition and it behooves us to pay
our own way as we go along."

"We run the chance of being becalmed or attacked
by pirates," objected the captain.

"We must take that chance," Leonard answered
firmly.

As the *Ark* sailed south past the coast of Spain and
Gibraltar, the passengers and crew lugged their soggy
bedding and clothes up from below and spread them on
the deck to dry. Everyone was happy to be alive, even
those poor wretches who had been so seasick.

The *Ark* sailed on with a steady wind. Off Gibraltar
the lookout shouted, "Five pirate ships to larboard!" The
adventurers aboard wanted to chase them and fight, but

Leonard and the captain were more prudent. They changed the course to due west and headed for the Caribbean Islands, leaving the pirate ships behind. Before long, they overtook a school of hundreds of flying fish. Some fell on deck. Jed, the drummer boy, and another lad caught several which they cleaned and ate for supper.

Except for a midday calm, when the sails hung slack for an hour or two, the wind held. There were weeks of clear sailing with nothing visible but water and sky. Then, one day at sunset, the voyagers were delighted to see strange, tropical birds with long, white tails, flying overhead, a sign that land was near.

Next morning the lookout called, "Land ho!"

Everybody came running on deck. Leonard tripped on Father White's long, black robe as they hurried up the companionway. While they watched, a dot of land on the horizon gradually changed as if by magic into a green island. As the *Ark* sailed nearer, the men could see brilliant flowers, exotic trees and plants growing to the water's edge.

When the *Ark* finally dropped anchor in a harbor off the island of Barbados in the West Indies, Leonard Calvert and the colonists went ashore to stretch their legs on solid ground. How sweet the earth smelled after the many days at sea! They ate sweet guavas, the ripe hearts of the cabbage palm dipped in pepper, yams, and, as for pineapples, they could not get enough. Father White wrote back to England:

> The Pineapple excells all the other fruits that I have tasted anywhere in the world: It is of a golden color . . . it has a spicy taste, which, as nearly as I can guess, is like that of strawberries mixed with sugar and wine.

While the colonists were still ashore on Barbados, they were overjoyed to see the little *Dove,* accompanied by the *Dragon,* sail into the harbor.

The colonists ran to the shore, shouting and waving; many were weeping with joy.

"Praise be to God," said Father White.

The men from the *Dove* came ashore as fast as the small landing boat could bring them.

"We never thought to see you again in this world," said Leonard, embracing the captain. "What happened?"

"We never could have ridden out the storm. Our ship and the *Dragon* turned back to the safety of an English harbor, where we waited until the storm died down. Then we set sail again, and here we are," the captain explained.

That was a night of rejoicing, feasting, drinking, and very little sleep.

When the *Ark* and the *Dove* were loaded with fresh water, seed corn, and potatoes, the two ships sailed on, together once again. They stopped briefly to visit other Caribbean Islands. At some of the smaller islands, natives paddled out to the ships in canoes to trade melons, bananas, and pumpkins for knives, bells, and other trinkets.

Lord Baltimore had warned them to stay away from Virginia, but Leonard decided to risk making a stop at Point Comfort to deliver a letter from the King and gifts to the Governor. The Virginians gave them a cordial welcome, hardly the reception they had expected. The whole nine days' visit was a pleasant one. Even Captain Claibourne, who had been so unkind to George Calvert, the First Lord Baltimore, was polite. However, he did try to frighten the colonists with tales of Indians waiting fully armed to kill them all as soon as they landed in their colony. Over the wine glasses at the Governor's table, Claibourne told Leonard of bloody Indian massacres in Virginia, where villages had been burned to the ground, men and women scalped, and children carried away.

When the colonists left Virginia, they took Captain Fleet with them to serve as a guide and interpreter. Fleet was a Virginia fur trader who knew the local Indian languages. When at last the *Ark* and the *Dove* sailed up the Chesapeake Bay, colonists eagerly watched the shore line. Maybe Claibourne had exaggerated about the Indians, but George Calvert had told the truth about the Bay. It was indeed beautiful. Father White wrote to friends in England, "In this long wished for country the forests are not disfigured with swamps, but firm land on either side of the bay. Fine groves of trees appear, not choked with undergrowth, but growing as if planted by the hand of man."

On the shores, east and west, Indians stood watching the ships. It was enough to make a man shiver in his boots. At night, signal fires dotted the forest like stars in a black sky. But at dawn the next morning the warriors had disappeared, and the colonists felt braver.

The ships nosed into a protected harbor and dropped anchor. Several men waded ashore to a small island which Father White named St. Clement's, after one of his favorite saints. The Captain ordered the shallop lowered for the women who had been pestering him to let them go ashore to wash the dirty linens. Scarcely had the boat pulled away from the *Ark* when it overturned, dumping the screeching women and the linens in the shallow water. The sailors saved the women, and as much of the linen as they could, for both were scarce in the New World.

After the shallop was bailed out, Leonard, Father White, and the captain rowed ashore. Father White knelt in a prayer of thanksgiving. The long voyage was over at last.

On March 25, 1634, the colonists planted a tall cross, which the men had made of tree trunks. Father White said solemn Mass. With great emotion, Governor Calvert took possession of the land in the name of King Charles I and Lord Baltimore.

5

St. Mary's, the First Town

AT SUNUP, LEONARD CALVERT, Captain Fleet, and a crew
set out in the *Dove,* leaving the *Ark* at St. Clement's.
They were on their way to make friends with the Indians,
as Lord Baltimore had instructed. Although there were
no Indians in sight as the pinnace sailed along the Potomac River, Governor Calvert felt sure that curious red
men were watching from behind the trees and bushes
that lined the tidy banks.

Looking up at the bellying sails, he said to Captain
Fleet, "I hope the breeze will hold until we reach the
Indian village you call Pascataway. I would give my hand
in friendship to the Emperor before nightfall."

"Take care that you address him as the Tayac,"
warned Captain Fleet. "That is the Indian word for
emperor."

Luckily, a light breeze held all day and just at sun-
down the *Dove* dropped anchor in a cove near Pascataway
Village. The colonists had come looking for Indians, and
here they were. Five hundred warriors, armed with long

bows, lined the shore. It was an awesome sight to the English.

Captain Fleet broke an arrow, the sign that the colonists had come in peace. At once, the Emperor and three braves paddled out to the ship and came aboard. In the Captain's cabin, after a greeting, the Governor said to Fleet, the interpreter, "Tell the Tayac we wish to be friends always and ask him for permission to settle in his country."

Fleet spoke slowly. Then the Tayac, brave and tall, a cape of beaver fur thrown across his bare shoulders, drew himself to full height. With arms folded, he answered in Algonquin, the language of the Pascataways, "Sit down wherever you please in my land."

On shore, the warriors became fearful for the safety of their leader, out of sight on the strange ship. They murmured among themselves, and one shouted a high note, like the cry of a wild bird. To reassure his people, the Tayac came out on deck and raised his hand to tell them all was well. The warriors soon lost their fears, and some were bold enough to swim out to the *Dove* and come aboard, climbing up the anchor chain, water dripping from their dark-skinned bodies. They walked about the deck, wondering at the bigness of the ship, admiring the heavy cannon. One stepped close to Governor Calvert, touched his white lace collar, then stooped to examine the shiny buckles on his boots. Another, laughing, pointed to the Captain's black beard and his wide-brimmed hat.

That night, after the Indians had gone ashore,

Leonard slept soundly as a bear. Now he knew the Indians were friends.

The next day the *Dove* returned to St. Clement's. Then, since St. Clement's did not have a good harbor, and Leonard was determined to find one, the *Ark* and the *Dove* once again weighed anchor. Fleet, aboard the *Ark,* guided the ships down the Potomac River to where it widened into the Bay. Here, they entered another river, then sailed north, stopping at a beautiful harbor. Two bays formed an anchorage large enough for three hundred ships.

"Surely no place could be better than this," Leonard said. "No place in England or all of Europe can equal it!"

Fleet spoke up. "Not so fast," he cautioned. "First you had better get permission from the chief of the Yoacomicoe Indians. His village lies on the other side of the river."

The *Ark* and the *Dove* sailed across the wide river and anchored close to a sandy point. Leonard, his brother George, and Captain Fleet landed and walked along the shore until they came to the Indian village. Two rows of bark houses stood on a gentle rise of land, overlooking a lovely bay shaped like a crescent moon.

The chief of the Yoacomicoes received them with dignity and listened to their resquest. He was willing to sell them land, for it so happened that the Yoacomicoes were planning to move away to a safer place, out of the warpath of the Susquehannocks, their enemies to the north.

Governor Calvert gave the Indians axes, hoes, hatchets, and many yards of cloth in payment for the land.

"Here we will build the first Maryland town," said Father White, when the Governor returned with the good news. "Let us call this town St. Mary's."

And everybody agreed.

Governor Calvert announced jubilantly, "This calls for a celebration and a feast in honor of St. Mary's." The colonists greeted his suggestion with cheers and shouts.

They shot off their cannon, to the astonishment of the Indians, who were proud to be friends with men who could make such loud thunder. Surely the Susquehannocks would keep their distance now! Always delighted with a feast, the Indians brought wild turkeys, partridge, oysters, squirrels, and corn bread. Their women gathered wood, and lighted fires. Soon there was a delicious smell of roast turkey in the forest.

After the feast, when everybody was full of good food and good will, the Indians offered to move from half of their homes in the village and let the colonists live in them until new houses could be built. The colonists were grateful for shelter against the weather and the forest, full of wild animals. Then, on top of this generous gift, the Indians gave the white men their gardens, already planted with corn, for they were farmers not warriors.

Leonard Calvert said to Father White, "I wonder what my brother Cecil will say when he hears we have a roof over our heads and gardens all planted, on our first day at St. Mary's?"

"This is the finger of God. Some great good is meant toward this people," answered Father White.

The Indian village was much like a small English village. Houses lined one side of a main street, and opposite lay the gardens, a patchwork quilt of leaf green, clay red, and earth brown. The houses, built of bark, were shaped like half-ovals. Some were as long as twenty feet. All were nine or ten feet high, with a wide hole in the center of the roof, to let out smoke from the fire below and let in light from the sun.

In the next weeks, as the braves showed the colonists how to dig for clams and where to look for wild turkeys and deer, the Indian women made friends with the English women. Instead of being quiet and shy, as they were in the presence of the men, they chattered and laughed while showing their new friends how to grind corn into meal and crack corn to make hominy.

The colonists, following the directions of Lord Baltimore, selected the place for their fort on a bluff at the mouth of Key Swamp. The site overlooked the town and could guard against approaches from both land and sea. Next, the leaders made a plan for the town, giving to each settler the land due him.

Governor Calvert chose for himself one hundred acres northwest of the fort on Mattaponi Path, the trail that led to another Indian village nine miles away. He reserved a large tract of land close by for his old friends, the Brents. Mistress Margaret Brent, her sister, and two brothers still planned to come to Maryland, once the colony was well under way.

North of the Governor's holdings, land was set aside for Father White's chapel. Still further north, on the east side of Mattaponi Path, was to be St. Peter's Freehold, future home of Thomas Cornwallis, Esq. From the very beginning, Cornwallis was a leader in Maryland, second only to Leonard Calvert.

As soon as a storehouse was built within the acreage where the fort would be, the colonists raised two flags— of England and of the Calvert family. They then brought their belongings from the *Ark* and the *Dove,* and settled down. The feeling in the town was so peaceful that Governor Calvert doubted they would ever need the fort. However, since the Proprietary had directed, "Build a fort at once," Leonard ordered the men to cut down trees and strip them. Soon the palisades began to go up: hewn logs, upright, close together, and sharply pointed on top.

In the town of St. Mary's, timber-frame houses were started.

Everybody worked, from Leonard Calvert to Jed, the drummer boy. Even gentlemen adventurers who had never done a day's work before, had blisters on their hands from swinging axes and sawing wood.

Then out of a clear sky, a worry edged its way into St. Mary's. Although the Indians were no longer living at St. Mary's, they had been coming back to town with gifts, venison, and wild turkeys. Then there were no more friendly visits; no one knew why.

The colonists became uneasy. Fearing an attack, they stopped building homes and pitched in to finish the fort. After a while they found out why the Indians had turned against them. Their former guide, Captain Fleet, who had returned to Virginia, and his friend, William Claibourne, had been spreading ugly rumors. According to these stories, the Marylanders really were Spaniards, planning to take the Yoacomicoes captive.

The settlers made no attempt to fight the Indians, but worked steadily building their town. In time, the Indians realized that the words of Fleet and Claibourne must have been lies. Before long they drifted back to St. Mary's, bringing deer meat and wild fowl as a peace offering. The colonists were glad to see them again, for by now they thought of the Yoacomicoe Indians as Marylanders like themselves.

Leonard Calvert was proud to write to his brother, Lord Baltimore, telling him that St. Mary's, after a few

months, was further advanced than Plymouth or Jamestown had been at the end of a year.

> Our success, dear brother, is due to your vision and
> careful planning, to our father's costly experience
> in *NewFoundLand,* and to the generous help of the
> Maryland Indians. I assure you we will not go hun-
> gry during the winter, for the forest is full of game
> and wild turkeys. Besides, we now have, on the edge
> of town, a mill for grinding corn, and, thanks to
> our friends, the Indians, there is always plenty of
> corn to grind.

At the end of the letter, a long one, Governor Calvert
described the fort:

> We have seated ourselves within a one-half mile of
> the river within a palisade of one hundred twenty
> yards square with four flanks. We have mounted
> one piece of ordnance and placed six murderers
> [cannons] in parts convenient, a fortification we
> think sufficient to defend against any such weak
> enemies as we have reason to expect here.

The letter traveled to England aboard the *Ark,*
which carried a load of beaver furs, dried corn, and salt
fish from Plymouth Colony, with which Maryland colonists traded. Leonard also sent along souvenirs of Maryland for Lord Baltimore to show at Court: an Indian
basket, beautifully woven of grass dyed with berries and
bark; several arrowheads traded from further west; and
a necklace of wampum for Lady Anne.

6

Father White and the Indians

FATHER WHITE AND NICOATUCAN, his Indian helper, were hard at work making one of the Indian houses into a temporary church. They set up a wooden altar and decorated the bark walls behind it with branches from the forest and a rose-and-silver-thread hanging brought from England. Father White placed the cross and candlesticks on the altar, then knelt in prayer. The prayer was a short one as there was still much to be done. He rose, crossed himself, and took up his hammer.

Nicoatucan crossed himself, too, and laughed. Father White laughed with him because he knew there was no irreverence in the childlike Indians.

Before the twigs and chips had been cleared away, the Catholic colonists began to assemble for Mass. Leonard and George Calvert, Jerome Hawley, Thomas Cornwallis, Edward and George Wintour, and others came in quietly and knelt on the hard earthen floor. After a long silence, Father White began to celebrate the Mass, while Nicoatucan and a group of Indians watched curiously from the door. Although they could not understand the Latin words, they were religious people and quickly grasped the idea that this was the way the colonists worshiped their god.

At the end of the service, Governor Leonard Calvert stepped to the altar, laid his hand on the Bible and promised to uphold the ideals and instructions of his father, the First Lord Baltimore. In Maryland, all men, Catholics and Protestants alike, would have the freedom to worship as they chose. No other colony in America was this free. In Virginia, a man could be hanged for his religious beliefs, and he fared little better in Plymouth.

Now that the church was established at St. Mary's, Father White wanted to fill it with Indians. Since they were too timid to come to him, he decided to go to them. Under Father White's direction, Nicoatucan and an Indian interpreter loaded a small pinnace with "a little chest of bread, cheese, corn, beans and a little flour . . . another chest carrying wine for religious purposes, holy

water for baptism, a box of sacred vessels, and a slab for the altar." There was also another casket full of the trifles the Indians liked: little bells, combs, knives, fish-hooks, needles, and thread. And, of course, Father White and his Indian friends took along a tent, for use in bad weather, and bows, arrows, and spears, for hunting.

At sunrise, while the mist was still on the river, they set sail, heading north on the Potomac. Three blue herons watched solemnly from the bank, and a loon called from the marshes.

The first night, the travelers visited a village near the mouth of the Wicomico River. The next night they spent at Port Tobacco, thirty miles further north. Wherever they stopped, the natives were drawn to Father White, for he was gentle and kind. He spoke with them, learning an Indian word or two and teaching them English words in exchange.

While Father White was visiting the Pascataways, still further north, their Tayac fell ill. Medicine men gave

him bitter-tasting potions, brewed from herbs and bark. They danced around his bark house, shrieking and making loud noises with their rattles to drive away the evil spirits. But instead of curing the patient, this treatment made him worse.

Father White asked, "Would the Tayac let the missionary try to cure him?"

The Tayac, fearing that he was going to die, agreed. For many days, Father White stayed with the sick man, giving him simple medicines brought from England. He nursed him gently and prayed, "May he live, O God, if it so please Thee."

When the Tayac began to get well, he was grateful to Father White. The priest was a better medicine man than the Indians. Perhaps his god was more powerful than the god of the Indians. The Tayac said, "Father, tell me about your god."

Father White told him some of the wonderful stories from the Bible: about Adam and Eve, Moses and the flight from Egypt, Noah and the Flood. The Tayac nodded. He knew about the Flood. It was in the Indian legends, too. The Tayac would have listened until morning. He urged his friend to make his home with them, but Father White knew it was time for him to return to his own people. As he left Pascataway Village, the missionary said, "Come to visit us at St. Mary's, and bring your family and all your tribe."

"We will come," replied the Tayac. "One day you will see us again."

As soon as Father White reached home, he and Governor Calvert put their heads together over Lord Baltimore's plan for the permanent church. In their enthusiasm they could see the building all finished, made of red brick and in the shape of a cross. The Governor pictured well-dressed, well-fed colonists sitting stiffly in the pews. Father White pictured them on their knees, and the church aisle crowded with Indians.

Work went along briskly, with everybody in town wanting to help. Those who could not bake bricks or lay them stood around giving advice and getting in the way. One evening, when the roofers were calking around the chimney, Leonard Calvert turned to Father White: "Methinks my brother, Lord Baltimore, will be pleased with this chapel, the first Catholic Church in the New World. It was he who ordered it and right smart he was to see our need so far ahead."

Father White replied, "Let us not forget that Lord Baltimore told us that this Catholic chapel was to be used by the Protestants as well." He thought a moment, then added, a smile crinkling his sensitive face, "I hope the Protestants wipe their feet before they enter God's House."

The Protestants did wipe their feet, and everybody worked together peacefully until the Devil got in and tripped up one Thomas Gerard, a Catholic with no use for tolerance. One morning, Gerard, who lived nearby at St. Clement's Manor, took home the keys to the chapel, so the Protestants could not get in to worship. When news of the incident reached the Governor's ear, he was quick to make Gerard bring back the keys, and fined him five hundred pounds of tobacco, to boot. This fine, grudgingly paid, was set aside to help pay the salary of Maryland's first Church of England minister, whenever that gentleman should arrive from England.

During the next few years, the new church was busy every day of the week. A wedding, baptism, or a funeral would bring the good people together. On Sundays the pews were filled with worshiping colonists, but only a few Indians came. As Father White went about his duties in the parish, he often thought about the Indians, especially the Tayac. He wished that he could talk with the Indian chief again, for by now the priest knew many more words of the Indian language.

The Tayac must have been thinking of Father White, too, for one day he arrived at St. Mary's with his wife, children, and enough members of the tribe to fill several log canoes.

Over a pipe, the Tayac again asked questions about the Christian religion. Father White set aside all other duties and spent long hours with the Indian leader, telling him about Jesus Christ and His gospel of love for all people. The Tayac listened attentively, his black eyes shining. After a time he said to Father White, "If I become a Christian I wish to wear clothes like Governor Calvert."

When the priest assured him that his wish would be granted, the Tayac swelled out his chest like a bullfrog.

Father White was pleased, too, for with their Tayac a Christian, many other Indians would follow his example.

Early in the morning of the Feast of Pentecost, the seventh Sunday after Easter, the Tayac dressed his magnificent, bronze body in one of the Governor's white, ruffled shirts and a pair of knee breeches. The hat he wore proudly, but not even the shiny, silver buckles could tempt him to try on the boots.

Everybody for miles around St. Mary's turned out for the baptism of the Tayac. Every seat in the chapel was taken, and now at last the aisle was crowded with Indians.

7

"We Make the Laws"

AFTER THE HARVEST had been gathered, Governor Calvert called together the freemen of the colony. When they
were seated before him, bolt upright, with wide, black
hats on their heads, the Governor said, "Gentlemen, at
this first Maryland Assembly of 1634, we are met to
ratify the laws, proposed by Lord Balitmore, for the governing of Maryland."

Thomas Cornwallis, one of the Commissioners, rose
to his feet, removed his hat, and addressed the Governor:
"I for one, object to ratifying these laws. Freemen of
Maryland should be allowed to make their own laws."

"Hear! Hear!" called out several other colonists.

Whereupon Governor Calvert rapped the table for
order. "One at a time, gentlemen, one at a time!"

During the heated argument that followed, the secretary broke his quill pen in his frantic haste to write down
all that was said, and he had to stop and sharpen another.

When the debate quieted down, Leonard explained
that the Maryland charter gave the Proprietary the right

to make the laws. The colonists shook their heads. They objected, and continued to do so until the Governor agreed to convey their objections to Lord Baltimore. It was not an easy letter for Leonard to write because he felt a loyalty to his brother as well as to Maryland.

When the letter reached Cecil Calvert, he was very angry. "How dare those men dictate to me the way to run my colony," he said to his wife, Anne.

"If only you could be there to handle things yourself, m'Lord."

"More than anything I want to be there, but I cannot leave England now, with Claibourne petitioning the King to give him Kent Island." He paced the floor. "When this same question of self-government came up at Jamestown, the King revoked the Virginia charter. I must not decide in haste or anger lest we lose Maryland's charter. I will take my time. Meanwhile, we must stop Claibourne. He still keeps the trading post at Kent Island against the King's orders, knowing as well as I do the Virginia charter has been revoked. My brother writes of him in each letter. Claibourne knows the island is ours, yet he pays no attention to my authority and stirs up the Indians against us."

While he was still angry, Lord Baltimore wrote a letter to Leonard: "If William Claibourne will not acknowledge the Maryland charter, seize him and detain him a close prisoner at St. Mary's, and take possession of his plantation on the Isle of Kent."

When Leonard received Cecil's letter six weeks

later, he shook his head, and said to himself, it is easier to sit in England and write such a letter than it is to catch a fox in the wilderness. Nevertheless, he sent word to Claibourne to stop trading in Maryland waters without authority from Lord Baltimore. As Claibourne kept on doing as he pleased, the Marylanders seized a pinnace belonging to him.

Now the fight was on. Claibourne promptly armed his own ship, the *Cocatrice,* and sailed to the Pocomoke River where he met the *St. Helen* and the *St. Margaret,* commanded by Thomas Cornwallis. Shots were fired on both sides. One shot took the life of the captain of the *Cocatrice,* a blow which brought the fight to a swift end. Although Maryland won this naval battle, Claibourne himself was still free. Before long, Governor Calvert heard that Claibourne had slipped off to England. Although nothing was settled, there was a short period of peace.

During this peaceful time, a ship arrived from England bringing the wives and daughters of Maryland landowners. They brought a few luxuries: silver, linens, and even a spinet or two. Among the gentlewomen were Mistress Margaret Brent, her sister, Mary; and Giles and Fulke, her two brothers. As soon as Margaret Brent's foot touched shore, St. Mary's sat up and took notice, for she was a strong woman, with a mind of her own and a quick way of expressing it. The Brents, close friends of Leonard Calvert, settled just east of his home, at a place called Sisters Freehold, in honor of the Brent sisters.

Soon, everyone in town was giving a party. The women hung up their linsey-woolsey dresses of dark color, and donned the gowns brought for them on the ship from London. They were of silk brocade and velvet, trimmed with spangled lace. For the first time, the tinkling sound of the spinet and the sweet notes of the flute were heard in Maryland.

Whenever Governor Calvert stopped in at Sisters Freehold to talk with Giles Brent about local affairs and to catch up on news of England, Margaret Brent listened and spoke her convictions. She was interested to hear from Leonard that during the second Assembly of 1638, Maryland freemen had won the right to make their own laws, subject to Lord Baltimore's veto. She nodded and smiled when Calvert read aloud from his brother's letter:

> "Offenders in murders, felonies and like mischiefs are to suffer such pains or fines as they would have suffered in like kinds in England. However, in Maryland, fines are to be paid in tobacco."

"It seems to me," she said, "if a man sows, cultivates, reaps, and cures his own tobacco he will think twice before breaking the law and losing all his labor."

Leonard and Giles agreed with her, and they all felt that Cecil Calvert had been wise to give the men of Maryland the freedom to make their own laws.

Meanwhile, in England, Lord Baltimore himself was not so sure. He was impatient to have first-hand news of his colony. As he still did not dare leave England, he wrote to Leonard, asking him to come to England for a visit. "Bring with you a red bird that I may see one with my own eyes," he said, at the end of the letter.

Leonard lost no time making plans for this trip. He appointed his friend, Giles Brent, Acting Governor to take his place while he was away and look after the affairs of the colony. Finally, when everything was in order, he sailed on the next ship for England.

Lord Baltimore was happy to see his brother after eight years.

"I caught a red bird," explained Leonard, "but a stupid servant let it go just before I set sail. However, I did bring one thing you asked for. Look in this pouch. It is the good red earth of Maryland."

Lord Baltimore rubbed the earth between his fingers and smiled. "Tell me all you can about Maryland," he said, "for I am hungry for news of my colony."

All evening, Leonard talked about Maryland, bringing St. Mary's, the Indians, the Bay, and even Kent Island into the room.

"How I wish my dear wife, Anne, had lived to hear you tell all of these stories. We spoke of Maryland often and were sure that someday both of us would see it," said Cecil sadly.

"At least you must come," Leonard replied.

Lord Baltimore pulled his chair close to Leonard's and lowered his voice. "There are many things I dare not write, brother," he said. "As you must know, there is a growing conflict between the King and his supporters, the Royalists, on one side, and Parliament and the

Roundheads, those short-haired Puritans, on the other."

Without warning, Cecil rose and held up his hand for silence. He went to the door and opened it carefully, peering into the dark hall. As he returned to his chair, he said, "I wanted to be sure that no one was listening at the keyhole. We Calverts are King's men, but, forsooth, I wish we had a stronger king than Charles the First. At any time he may be toppled from the throne. To save our colony, and maybe even my life, I must be careful to keep peace with both sides."

Leonard shook his head. "And I thought we had troubles at home," he said.

Cecil looked up with a quick smile. "How it warms my heart to hear you call Maryland home. Father would have liked that."

He pulled his heavy oak chair closer to the fire. "To get back to our problems," he continued, "there is, as you may know, a penal law which goes back to Queen Elizabeth's time, against harboring Jesuit priests. So, in our letters, we must be very careful never to mention Father White or any of the other Jesuit priests in Maryland. From now on, when I write you, I will use a special code and refer to the priests as 'those of the hill,' or use the title 'Mister' instead of 'Father.' "

"I understand, brother," Leonard replied, "but such a law is a crime. The Jesuit priests we now have in the colony are making friends for us among the Indians and helping to keep peace in Maryland. In the nearby colonies, the Indians kill the settlers and burn the villages."

Lord Baltimore sat silently for a moment and then said, "With you in Maryland and me here, we will keep the peace in both places, God willing."

Leonard stood up. "I see I must return to Maryland alone, although I had hoped to take you with me. You have your troubles with Parliament and the Roundheads, and I have Claibourne. I wish you Godspeed."

Across the sea in the colonies, people were divided in their loyalties between Roundheads and Royalists. New England favored Parliament, while Maryland and Virginia sided with the King. Leonard came home from England to find Maryland a hornet's nest. Captain Richard Ingle, a Roundhead, had sailed into St. Mary's harbor where he had spoken boldly against the King. He was promptly arrested for treason and detained on his own ship. When the guard was changed, Ingle escaped, vowing vengeance on Maryland.

Now Maryland had two enemies, Claibourne and Ingle. No one knew for certain whether these men were working together or not, but at the very same time that Claibourne was recapturing Kent Island, Ingle sailed into St. Mary's harbor in an armed vessel and seized the town. He and his men set fire to houses, burned the early records of the colony, and stole the Great Seal, used on state papers. Ingle sent kind Father White to England in chains, the good man's only crime being that he was a Jesuit priest. Most of the townspeople of St. Mary's took refuge in the fort.

Mistress Margaret Brent stayed at home. No one,

not even Ingle, dared destroy Sisters Freehold with Mistress Brent standing defiantly in the hall, her hands on her hips. However, one bold upstart did take the hinges from her door, and used the door to make a fire for roasting some of her cattle for supper.

Governor Leonard Calvert, knowing that he could do nothing against the enemy without help, fled to Virginia to see if he could raise an army. Although the Virginians had little love for Maryland, some were willing to fight for money. As soon as Leonard had recruited sufficient forces, promising to pay the soldiers well, out of his own pocket, he landed in Maryland with his army. He lashed into Ingle, drove him out of St. Mary's, and then chased Claibourne off Kent Island. Whereupon, both Claibourne and Ingle fled to England.

Within a few months after this victory, Leonard became ill and died. The colonists mourned him sincerely as a friend and as a strong Governor. He had served Maryland well during thirteen difficult years. On his deathbed, he named Thomas Greene Acting Governor, and Margaret Brent executor of his estate.

Mistress Brent was honored, but, at the same time, she found that she had been given a hard task. Although Leonard Calvert had been a good Governor for many years, he had been so busy, generously serving Maryland, that he had saved little money for himself. The Virginia soldiers were demanding their back pay. Margaret Brent gave them all that Leonard had left, and paid the rest of the debt with corn, cows, and tobacco belonging to Cecil

Calvert, the Lord Proprietary. This was a very bold step.

When Lord Baltimore heard of it, he was furious to think that a woman had been so free with his property, and he said so in an angry letter to the Assembly.

To Margaret Brent's surprise, the Assembly stood by her, replying indignantly to His Lordship's letter:

> "We do verily believe that it was better for the colony's safety to be in her hands than in any man's else in the whole Province . . . for the soldiers would never have treated any other with that civility and respect."

For Mistress Brent this was only the beginning. Now, as Leonard Calvert's executor, she came to the Assembly, where, to the astonishment of the freemen, she asked for the right to vote. A woman asking for a vote! What was the world of 1647 coming to? The men shook their heads, and Acting Governor Greene replied with a loud, firm "No!"

8

Puritans and Politics

WHEN CECIL CALVERT read the letter from the Maryland Assembly defending Margaret Brent, he crumpled it and threw it on the floor in anger. Then he hesitated, bent down, picked it up, and smoothed it out, his anger gone. This was no time to indulge in hurt pride. Maryland had been served well by Mistress Brent, and that was good. If only his brother had lived! Thomas Greene was not the man to take his place as Governor of Maryland. No doubt Green was honest and a loyal friend of Leonard's, but not a strong enough man for such a responsible position. It will take a wise man to lead Maryland during these troubled times, Cecil thought.

Lord Baltimore paced the floor, going over names of possible governors for his colony. Should he choose Cornwallis? Wintour? Giles Brent? If his own son, Charles, were old enough to govern, there would be no question. In time, Charles would be Governor and Lord Proprietary. Cecil wished the boy were home from Oxford, so they could talk together.

Cecil paced the floor, thinking. After a time, he said aloud, "Stone is the man. William Stone knows our colony and he knows Virginia." This appointment would be a wise move, for he is a Protestant and friendly toward Parliament. At present there is no telling which way the wind will blow.

Lord Baltimore wrote the letter to the Assembly, appointing William Stone Governor of Maryland. He signed his name with a flourish, CECIL CALVERT, LORD PROPRIETARY, and stamped the document with the Great Seal of Maryland. It was a handsome new silver seal, like the first one which had been lost during Ingle's Rebellion. The Calvert arms and the Crossland arms of his mother's family, were topped by the crown of England. Cecil picked it up and read aloud the Calvert family motto, written in Italian: *Fatti Maschi Parole Femine* ("Manly in deeds, womanly in words"). Cecil wished he had a chance for deeds. He sighed. Would the day ever come when he could go to Maryland instead of talking about it? He turned the seal over. On the other side there was a knight in full armor, and on the rim was inscribed, "Cecil Calvert, absolute master of Maryland and Avalon, Baron of Baltimore." Enough to make any man proud.

Before night, Lord Baltimore had dispatched the letter and seal. By the end of the week they were on shipboard headed for Maryland. And so it was that William Stone became the Governor of Maryland in the year 1648.

The new Governor found many problems; the thorniest was that of the Puritans. Since the beginning of the Virginia colony, a group of Puritans had lived there. As time went on, more and more of them came from England. The Virginians in power liked neither the Puritans' religion nor their increasing numbers.

The Puritans thought that they were right and everyone else was wrong. Plain living was holy, they maintained; fine clothes, music, dancing, and all luxuries were sinful. They thought the elaborate form of worship in the Church of England was just as bad as the ritual in the Catholic churches. The hymns, vested clergy, music, and responses the Puritans labeled "popish."

When Lord Baltimore heard that no other colony wanted the Puritans, he, being a man of tolerance, invited them to come to Maryland. This was sound business as well, for new settlers meant more crops, and more crops meant a wealthier colony. The Puritans turned down the first invitation, but when Governor Stone dispatched a second invitation, they accepted. They had no choice, for they had to leave Virginia and had nowhere else to go. They streamed into Maryland, three hundred

strong, and settled in a town called Providence at the head of the Chesapeake Bay.

That same year, 1649, news reached Maryland that Charles I had been beheaded. England was now a Commonwealth under the Puritan, Oliver Cromwell, who had led the revolt against the established Church of England. Greene, Acting Governor while Governor Stone was temporarily absent from the colony, made a big blunder. Following the example of the Governor of Virginia, he pledged the allegiance of Maryland to Charles II, as King of England, instead of to Cromwell.

As soon as Governor Stone returned, he tried to set things right by belatedly changing allegiance to the Commonwealth, but the damage had already been done. The Puritans in Providence, who had supported Cromwell all along, were so angry with Maryland that they wanted to fight.

When Lord Baltimore heard about Greene's blunder, he was almost as angry as the Puritans, for he feared he might lose his colony. In an effort to reassure the Puritans, he told Stone to call an Assembly at once, to pass a law about religion. The Toleration Act, which was passed in 1649, turned out to be less tolerant than the first instructions of George and Cecil Calvert. On the good side, it forbade the calling of names: "no one was to be called a heritick, idolitor, Puritan or Popish Priest." Any name caller had to apologize in public to the person offended, and pay a fine. Another clause was enacted, saying that anyone who did not believe in the Holy Trinity

—Father, Son, and Holy Ghost—could be punished by death, and his estate forfeited. This was a long step backward from the religious toleration practised so successfully in the colony for its first fifteen years, but as it turned out, Maryland very seldom enforced this harsh law.

By this time, the Puritans were more interested in power than in tolerance. They wanted to make everyone believe what they believed. To stir up trouble, they sent reports to Parliament that the Maryland colony did not give them religious freedom. This so angered Cromwell that he took Lord Baltimore's province away from him and appointed two royal commissioners to govern Maryland in Stone's place. One was Richard Bennett, an ardent Puritan of Providence, and the other, that old trouble maker, William Claibourne. Claibourne returned to the colony and lost no time in taking Kent Island for himself. In order to attain his ends, he changed his loyalties and politics with every change in power, being a Royalist or a Roundhead, whichever best suited his own interests.

In the two months that Bennett and Claibourne governed (May to June, 1652), they made themselves so unpopular that the colony was turned over to Stone again. Governor Stone, still loyal to Lord Baltimore, now had to take his orders from Cromwell. Whether he was backed by Cromwell or Lord Baltimore, the people at St. Mary's were glad to have him back in office.

The Puritans continued to rebel against Stone's authority until he decided to go to Providence himself, to settle the dispute, peacefully if possible. With one hundred and thirty men he set sail in twelve small ships. They carried no cannon. News of their coming traveled faster than they did, and the Puritans were ready for them.

The *Golden Lion,* a large ship with heavy guns, was waiting for the small ships. Governor Stone led his fleet up Herring Creek to get out of the range of the *Golden Lion.* Whereupon the *Golden Lion* blocked the entrance to the creek and fired on the defenseless ships. Quickly, Stone ordered his men to drop anchor and attack by land, using their own muskets, but the Puritans had thought of that, too. A much larger force marched against Stone's men, shouting, "In the name of God, fall on! God is our strength!"

Stone's men shouted, "Hey for St. Mary's!" and pushed ahead.

The battle was short and swift, ending with a victory for the Puritans. Although the victors promised mercy to all who surrendered, ten men were condemned to death. Governor Stone, who had been wounded, was one of the unfortunate ten.

Four went to their death. Just as the others were being led to their execution, Stone's wife, Virlinda, and several other women rushed up. They pled so eloquently for mercy that the Puritans' hearts were touched and they spared the lives of the remaining captives.

"Hey for St. Mary's! Praise be to God!" cried the grateful Marylanders.

Although Governor Stone's life was spared, his property and that of his followers was seized by the Puritans. Maryland was thrown into confusion. No one was certain who was governing. Business, trade, and industry —shipbuilding, tanning, barrel making—were affected. Even land agreements were threatened, and some people were afraid to plant the tobacco crop. The Puritans in Maryland were following the example of the Puritans in England, who, in their fanaticism, had destroyed church property and homes and put innocent people to death. At Durham Cathedral, where George Calvert and his friend, Toby Matthews, had played as children, ten thousand prisoners were held. These poor wretches burned all the beautiful wood carvings to keep from freezing to death.

Cromwell, now called "Protector of the Common-wealth," wanted no more violence. When word of the Puritan bloodshed and disorder in Maryland reached him, he was not pleased. He held a meeting with Lord Baltimore and decided that this wise man knew more about managing his colony than anyone else. Then and there he restored Cecil's rights as Lord Proprietary, writing to the Province: "Let things be in Maryland as they were before they were disturbed."

When the Puritans in Maryland heard this news, they could not believe their ears.

"After all our fighting for Cromwell, he hands Maryland back to that popish Lord Baltimore!" said one.

And another, "Everybody changes his opinion except us. The Puritans of Providence never change."

A third chimed in, "The next thing, they will try to make us shout, 'Hey for St. Mary's!' "

"They won't get Kent Island," said Claibourne.

Lord Baltimore now appointed a man named Josiah Fendall as the Governor, one of his few mistakes in judging character. Fendall wanted power for himself. In fact, he wanted to rule Maryland in place of the Lord Proprietary. To further this wish, he plotted to seize control of the Assembly. Luckily, before he could carry out his scheme, Lord Baltimore heard of it. He dismissed Fendall from office, and made his own brother, Phillip Calvert, Governor of Maryland.

It was during this time that Cromwell died, and the monarchy was restored to England.

Hail to King Charles II!

Once again the Puritans were out of favor in England, as well as in the colonies. With his old and loyal friend, Charles II, on the throne, Lord Baltimore hoped to catch his breath and rest a while. It had been an anxious time for him.

Shortly after King Charles was crowned, a ship came from Maryland to England, bringing to Cecil a cargo of tobacco and beaver skins and the two arrowheads to be paid to the King at Windsor Castle at Whitsuntide. Cecil fingered the arrowheads with great interest, for they brought his colony close to him. One was pure white, the other dark as onyx. What skillful artists the Indians must be, he thought. The white arrowhead, chipped to a slender point, was perfectly balanced. The dark one, larger by half, was shaped and polished like one of the crown jewels. Cecil recalled Leonard's last visit and his description of the Indians of Maryland, and the memory of his brother filled him with sorrow. He was tired. The weight of responsibility—protecting his colony in England and guiding it from across the sea—was heavy on him. He needed a change.

Lord Baltimore decided that he would take the arrowheads himself to King Charles II, instead of sending them by a messenger. Why not engage a barge and make the pleasant trip up the River Thames from London? So, accompanied by a lackey, Cecil set out. He was dressed in the new-fashioned greatcoat and waistcoat, the coat of black, lined all in crimson, and the waistcoat of blue brocaded stuff. A lace cravat at his neck matched the lace ruffles at his wrists. His hat was wide and black, and his shoes had silver buckles. A sword hung at his side, and his gloves were handsomely embroidered.

The sun sparkled on the river as the bargemen bent to their oars. Swans floated by. A patient horse plodded along the towpath, pulling a freight barge loaded with hogsheads of tobacco. Cecil wondered whether or not they were from his colony. Lawns stretched to the water's edge, and green willow trees swept the surface of the river. Cherry and apple trees and lilacs bloomed in many a garden, all white and pink and lavender. A lark made him think of his boyhood at Kiplin.

Presently the great, gray towers of Windsor Castle came into view, and the spires of Eton College, just across the river. Life was good. Next week his son, Charles, now a young man, would be home from Ireland with his bride. Perhaps, God willing, they could all go to Maryland together before the cold weather. . . .

9

The Governor in Residence

"HEAR YE, HEAR YE! Ship in sight. New Governor coming! Hear ye, good people of St. Mary's. Ship in sight. New Governor coming!" shouted the Town Crier, striding up and down Middle Street, ringing his brass bell.

Phillip Calvert, who had been Maryland's Governor during the year 1660–1661, was talking to his neighbor, Thomas Cornwallis, when the Town Crier passed his gate. The two gentlemen snatched up their black beaver hats from the settle in the hall and walked across the lawn to Chancellor's Point, where the ship would dock. Shielding their eyes with their hands, they watched the ship, a two-master under full sail. Already she was close enough to shore so they could see the King's colors flying.

At Sisters Freehold, Margaret Brent, in the middle of a long letter to a cousin in England, laid down her quill pen and called to her sister, who was sitting at her needlepoint frame, "Come, Mary, let us hasten to the wharf. Imagine Charles being Governor!"

Next door, on the plantation called The White

House, Giles Brent was riding a spirited horse. He had just come in the driveway after a gallop along Mattaponi Road. When he heard the news, he quickly wheeled his horse around and cantered down to the Point, followed by most of the dogs in town and half the small boys.

Katherine Stale, a Colonial housewife kneading dough, flour up to her elbows, hastily put the batch of dough on the hearth, wiped her hands on her apron, and ran out of the door of her house at the edge of town. She did not want to miss a thing. The smith drove the last nail in a horseshoe, laid down his hammer on the anvil, and headed for the Point. Two slaves in the fields looked up, and then went on hoeing the tobacco. Mothers with babies in their arms and small children clinging to their full skirts were the last to reach the wharf. By the time the ship docked, everybody was on hand, except one man in the stocks, another in the pillory, and the slaves.

When the ship tied up at the wharf, the new Governor and his lady were the first to step ashore. The men cheered lustily and the women waved their handkerchiefs and whispered to one another, "Look what she's wearing. That hooded cloak of green must be the new fashion in London."

Then, to the joy of the womenfolk, the Governor's lady threw back her hooded cloak.

The whispering grew to a buzzing. "Observe the pointed bodice and the slashed sleeves!"

Thomas Cornwallis gave the newcomers an affec-

tionate welcome. He bowed to Mistress Calvert and said to Charles, "I trust your father is in good health. We hope to see him step ashore before long."

Giles Brent dismounted. "Pray take my horse, Governor, and ride to your new home, the Palace of St. John's."

"I will not be the Governor until Uncle Phillip gives me the oath," corrected Charles, laughing. "It is kind of you to offer your horse, but we want to walk through the town and see everything. Besides, the solid earth feels good after six weeks at sea."

As he walked along the wharf, Charles noted with satisfaction the many wooden hogsheads of tobacco piled ready for loading on the ship. He realized, as never before, that land meant tobacco, and tobacco meant wealth.

The Governor's wife took his arm. "Look, Charles. Indians at the edge of the crowd, bronze men with straight, black hair. They're not painted at all. I thought Indians painted themselves most gaudily."

Thomas Cornwallis laughed. "It's easy to tell you are new to Maryland, ma'am, for everyone around here knows that Indians paint themselves only when going on the warpath. It's against the law to come into St. Mary's showing even one streak of paint."

They strolled past Sisters Freehold, with the townspeople trailing behind. Next they passed The White House, belonging to Giles Brent. Looking up the hill they saw the Fort of St. Mary's, with the iron cannons mounted at the corners.

Charles turned to Phillip. "I am right glad to see our murderers guarding the fort."

He walked on, thinking what a charming town it was, with the sixty houses strung along Middle Street. He was amazed to see so many houses with brick fronts and chimneys. He had expected to see nothing but log cabins with oiled paper in the windows. But many of these houses had glass windows like those in London. Since his wife was along, Charles did not stop at the tavern, thirsty as he was. As he passed the little brick Catholic chapel, he uncovered his head and said a short prayer, asking God to help him rule the colony.

The newcomers heard shouts and laughter. When they reached the top of the hill, they saw a group of boys and girls, dressed exactly like their parents and lined up in front of the stocks and pillory. The children were teasing the two men imprisoned there.

Charles stopped and questioned one unfortunate man. "What is your name?"

"Failing Williams, your honor," he answered, flushing.

"Pray tell me what brought you to this sorry state?"

"It wasn't because I ate Huddle Sparrow's pig, though I did eat it all, and gave away the chittlings and jowls, it was because I swore on the Bible it was my own pig, when I knew all along the ear slits showed the porker was his'n."

Charles wanted to hear more about the laws and penalties of the colony, but he knew his wife was eager to see her new home. Although the Palace of St. John's could not compare with the palaces in England, it was indeed a fine house, and as long as three town houses put together. Mistress Calvert liked the tall red chimneys outlined against the blue sky. She was pleased with the setting of the house on the green slope, surrounded by one hundred acres of rich land, bounded by water: St. Mary's Bay in front, St. John's Creek to the north, and, to the south, Mill Creek.

Once inside the house, she was charmed with the wide fireplaces, the mullioned windows, and the corner cupboard where she would put her Grandmother Darnell's dinner set. "My sideboard will go there, next to the window," she said to Charles, "with your new pewter tankards on top."

"There will be plenty of time for you to arrange your house," replied Charles. "Rest now, my dear, you must be tired after the long trip."

"Yes, I am tired, Charles, but I am charmed with

our new home," she said, as she started slowly up the graceful stairway.

This was a great day at St. Mary's. The people were torn between their interest in the new governor and the array of wares for sale on board ship. As soon as the wide front door closed behind the Calverts at the Palace of St. John's, everyone with a hogshead of tobacco to spend hurried back through the town and crowded onto the ship.

Here, spread out for all to see were silk and worsted bed curtains, Dutch linen sheets, spangled lace, brocades, velvets, dimities, and silks, pewter tankards and platters, a few stools and chairs, andirons, and, of course, tools. The women fingered the beautiful materials, while the men tried on the black hats, made from their own Maryland beaver skins.

"Don't spend too much," husbands cautioned wives, "quit rents are due."

"You don't expect us to wear old dresses to the Governor's party, do you?" the wives replied.

Before the week was out, the captain of the ship had sold every length of material he had brought from England.

Soon the wives of the colonists had made themselves fine dresses, copied after the new style worn by Mistress Calvert. Each had a pointed bodice, slashed sleeves, and a full skirt. And every woman who could afford it had a hooded cloak.

Since the beginning of the colony, the Feast of the

Assumption had been set aside as the day the quit rents, or land taxes, to the Lord Proprietary, were to be paid. It was the biggest holiday in Maryland, next to Christmas. As soon as Charles Calvert was sworn in as Governor (his Uncle Phillip becoming Deputy Governor), he was told that he was expected to give a party.

Preparation began at once. For weeks, Charles Calvert's thirty servants were busy. Margaret Brent sent over her excellent cook, Martha, to help.

On the day of the feast, trestle tables were set out under the trees and loaded with all sorts of good things to eat: fish, terrapin, roast wild turkeys, bear, and venison. Servants ran back and forth from the kitchen with hot corn bread, meat and oyster pies, steaming plum puddings, and sweetmeats. Syllabub, a delicious dessert made with sweet cream and wine, pleased the ladies. There were tankards of foaming ale and casks of red wine.

Men, women, and children had come by boat, horseback and oxcart, from all parts of the colony. Games of skill, dancing on the green, feasting, and gossiping made the payment of quit rents less painful. After the last colonist had gone, Charles looked at the hogsheads of tobacco and the bags of corn. He shook his head.

"If this barter system of payment goes on, we'll be buried in tobacco. We must have coins of our own. I'll bring the matter up at the next Assembly."

10

A Visit to England

CHARLES, FRESH FROM ENGLAND where legal matters were apt to be formal, pricked up his ears when the Maryland Assembly opened. In came two men dragging a dead wolf, his limp, gray tail trailing across the floor.

"We come to claim the bounty on this wolf," the men said, when they stood before the long council table.

The nine burgesses of the Lower House sniffed, and the aristocrats, the six counselors of the Upper House, took white handkerchiefs from their wide cuffs and held them to their long noses. Cornwallis remarked to the man seated on his left, "This wolf seems to be very dead, indeed."

Someone snickered, and one of the settlers in the back of the room said in a loud voice, "That is the selfsame wolf I shot a fortnight ago, and I collected the bounty for him, too."

As soon as the laughter died down, Governor Calvert leaned forward, "The selfsame beast? Are you sure?"

"Yes, Governor. I swear before God I'd recognize

the sneer on his ugly face anywhere, for he was me first wolf and I was right proud to bring him down. Night was coming on when I got him to my door, so I left him outside, thinking to skin him the next day. Come sunup, he was gone, not a trace of him anywhere, hide nor hair."

"May it please your Lordship and gentlemen of the Assembly," said Cornwallis, rising and removing his hat, "I move that from now on, we pay a bounty on a wolf head only. Upon payment of the bounty, we cut out the tongue, to make sure that one wolf head is not used twice."

"All agreed say, Aye. Opposed, No."

As there was not a single "No," the secretary wrote the new Wolfe Law into the Maryland records.

"Next case!"

Charles hoped this one would merit a fat fine, for more revenue was needed to build a jail and a court house.

A settler was led before him, a wheelwright accused of selling an Indian into slavery, a devilish mean crime. After weighing the evidence, the Governor pronounced the man guilty and fined him five hundred pounds of tobacco. The words were hardly out of his mouth when the secretary rose, cleared his throat, and read aloud the Maryland law concerning the stealing of Indians: "Whatsoever person shall steal friend Indian and sell him is punished by death."

The Governor had no choice but to abide by the

law. He nodded, and the unfortunate man was taken off to the gallows.

As soon as the scuffling by the door quieted down, the Assembly turned its attention to a man standing before the council table with his head bowed. It seems he had been heard swearing—by two persons.

"Did he blaspheme the name of God?" asked the Governor.

"We cannot rightly say he did, though his cursing was not for ladies." The accused was lucky, for he could have had a hole bored in his tongue if he had used the Lord's name in a curse. As it was, the punishment was light, a measly five pounds of tobacco, to be set aside for the new jail.

The case that followed concerned a crime on the high seas. A Captain Prescott had had a woman passenger hanged on shipboard as a witch, after accusing her of being the cause of a dreadful storm that nearly wrecked his ship.

"Witches!" said Governor Calvert indignantly. "There is no such thing as a witch. As this dreadful deed took place on the high seas, it comes under English law, not ours, and must be tried in England." Charles brought his fist down on the table in anger. "If the decision were mine, I'd hang the Captain!"

For two days, other local troubles were settled. A hog belonging to one man had rooted up corn belonging to another; a thief had broken into a storehouse and taken a barrel of ripe beer; a stone had gone through the Brents' glass window. Some said the Breen boy threw it, some said it was the Carter boy. The case was dismissed for lack of evidence.

Around noon on the third day of the Assembly, Charles Calvert had a chance to mention the coining of money. After haggling for an hour, the Assembly decided that Maryland would not use coins sent over from England by the Lord Proprietary, but would ask his Lordship's permission to set up a local mint where the colony could make its own coins.

Charles wrote to his father, stating the business of the colony which had been brought up at the Assembly. Then he told about his own family.

For the Right Honorable Cecil Calvert, Lord Baltimore, May it please your Lordship:

I am not in condition as yet to venture upon such a changeable design as a saw-mill which would

cost too much before it would yield a profit. . . .
Thank you, Father, for the summer suit you sent,
for the pewter platter and the copper stew pans full
of good yellow wax. . . . Fines be so small here, to
defray expenses of the Maryland Court I am forced
to entertain the council at my own expense here
at St. John's.

> Your Lordship's most dutiful son,
> Charles Calvert

Not long after the letter started on its way, sorrow
came to the young Governor. His wife died at the birth
of their first child, and the infant died also. When the sad
news reached England, Cecil sent Anne Calvert, a young
cousin, to act as hostess for Charles at the Palace of St.
John's. As she was a comely young woman with great
good sense, she attracted several suitors, and in a short
time she was married.

A charming widow, Jane Suwall, caught the eye of
the lonely Charles Calvert and soon became his second
wife. Jane persuaded her husband to move from the
Palace of St. John's to her beautiful home at Mattaponi.
This choice spot, one thousand acres of land on the
Patuxent River, was near Mattaponi Fort. Here, Charles
Calvert's son was born in 1667. The baby was called
Cecil after Lord Baltimore and nicknamed "Little Cis."

When the news reached Cecil Calvert, he was delighted. The thought of being a grandfather pleased
him, and he wished he might visit Maryland to see his

grandson. There was no chance of this, however, as his duties to his colony still kept him in England. But he thought to himself that he would write and invite Charles, his wife, and baby to visit him, as soon as the child was old enough to travel.

Cecil smiled, thinking of the little boy. He would tell his grandson all about the family. He would lift the child up to see the painting of his great-grandfather, George Calvert, the First Lord Baltimore, and show him the portrait of his grandmother, Lady Anne Arundel, painted when she was young and beautiful. Years ago, Cecil had promised Anne that he would have his own portrait painted to hang next to hers. Always he had been too busy. Perhaps, while his grandson was with him, they could be painted together. Yes, he liked the idea. He would send a message to the Court painter, Gerard Soest, right away, and arrange for the sittings.

When Governor Charles Calvert received his father's invitation, he could not leave Maryland. The colony was involved in two kinds of disputes, one about tobacco and the other about boundaries. Both had to be settled before he would feel free to leave. The Governor of Virginia had stirred up the people of his colony—and Maryland as well—by suggesting that no tobacco be planted for a whole year, in the hope of raising the price. The Lord Proprietary would have none of this plan. He wrote emphatically: "The rich will profit and the poor man will starve." Arguments went back and forth across the ocean, and between representatives from Virginia and

Maryland, but, as nothing could change Cecil's positive "No," the planting of tobacco went on as usual.

Cecil Calvert was interested in all people: Dutch, Italian, French, Catholic, Jew, Indian, Negro—rich or poor. To protect people in his colony, he wrote the Naturalization Law, which was more liberal than the Toleration Act. This law granted citizenship to colonists coming from other countries, as well as from England. This was a new idea in the world of 1666. Cecil stated of one of his colonists, a Hollander named Emperor Smith, "Know ye that we . . . do hereby declare him to be a free denizen of this, our Province of Maryland."

The Naturalization Law saved the life of Dr. Jacob Lumbrozo, a Jew whom another colony had sentenced to hang because of his religious beliefs. He fled to Maryland where, under Cecil's Naturalization Law, he became a citizen. As such, he could speak his beliefs without fear, for Maryland had remained tolerant, in practice, in spite of the Toleration Act.

More letters crossed the ocean from father to son. This time they concerned Maryland's boundary line.

Virginia had taken a slice of land in the south; the Dutch were claiming a wide section along the northern and eastern borders.

There had always been boundary trouble to the north. At the time of the founding of Maryland, Dutch settlers from Amsterdam were living there. After the Indians chased the Dutch away, the Swedes came along and made it their home. Then the Swedes moved on and the Dutch came back again, claiming that the land was theirs. However, Maryland did not acknowledge this claim.

When this dispute led to talk of war between the Dutch and the Maryland colonists, the Dutch sent two commissioners, Augustine Herman and Resolved Waldron, from New Amsterdam to Maryland to find out what the people and the Governor intended to do. As they traveled through the colony, Herman questioned everyone he met and found that the Marylanders were not inclined to fight. He began to like the place and the people. When Waldron returned to New Amsterdam, Herman stayed behind.

Augustine Herman, who came from Bohemia and settled in the New World, was a surveyor and a map maker. He wrote to Lord Baltimore, offering to draw an accurate map of Maryland in exchange for a grant of land.

Cecil was pleased. "A good map will help me to defend my rights," he said. He knew by heart the boundaries mentioned in his grant: "All lands north of Virginia, on both sides of the Chesapeake Bay, from the fortieth parallel to the mouth of the Potomac." But without a reliable map, he found it hard to know exactly how the boundary lines lay across the countryside.

As fast as ships could carry letters to England and back, the deal was settled. Herman was given five thousand acres of land on the Elk River, which he called Bohemia Manor. At once he began the survey for the map of Maryland.

Meanwhile, Charles Calvert had been going ahead with plans to take his family to England. There was only one drawback. "I hesitate to leave Uncle Phillip in my place, Father," he wrote, "because he is easily influenced. You must make it clear to him that he is to make no changes in government while I am away."

Accordingly, Cecil sent his brother, Phillip, written orders telling him what to do and what not to do while he was Acting Governor of Maryland.

In 1669, Charles, his wife, Little Cis, and a slave boy set sail. They were loaded down with gifts for grandfather: dried peaches, corn, a long tablecloth made of homespun flax, and two frisky, gray squirrels in a cage.

After three stops to pick up tobacco at river wharves, the ship headed for England. Outside the dangerous Capes they ran into rough weather. One heavy roll of the ship sent the squirrel's cage skittering across the deck. It turned over, the door flew open, and out scampered the two squirrels. One was soon cornered inside a coil of line and returned to his cage. The other one took to the rigging as though he had been an able seaman in His Majesty's Navy for fifteen years.

Deck hands swarmed up the rigging after the squirrel, who chattered and scolded, always just out of reach. He was never caught, but he apparently did not lack for food or drink. One seaman swore he saw a shadowy gray figure leaping from hogshead to hogshead as the ship was unloading near London. No one could be sure, for the crew had been issued a double portion of grog in celebration of the safe crossing.

The tale was fun to tell at dinner when the Calvert family was seated around the long table.

For the Calverts, young and old, the reunion in England was a joyous one. To the delight of the family, Gerard Soest caught the spirit of the visit in a beautiful painting, a full-length portrait like the one of the First Lord Baltimore. In it, the Second Lord Baltimore and his grandson stand side by side against a gray-green background, with the slave boy in the shadow behind the child. Warm rose red glows on the table cover and wall hanging.

Cecil Calvert is dressed in Maryland's colors: a gold cloth waistcoat, black coat, black stockings, and black ruffles at the knee. Little Cis wears a gold brocade dress reaching to the floor, with the tip of one toe showing. His sash and capelet are rose. How different the two faces are in every way—the boy's, round and young; Cecil's mature, sensitive, strong, framed by his shoulder-length, brown hair.

Cecil was proud of this portrait. Whenever anyone stopped in to see it, he always said, "The boy has his grandmother's fair complexion." Then quickly he would add, "Look closely. See the map I am holding in my hand? The boy holds it, too. That is the new map of Maryland made by Augustine Herman. It is one of the finest maps in the world."

I I

Rebellion

FOR THE NEXT FEW years after Governor Charles Calvert returned from England, things were calm in Maryland. Now and then, Indians from outside the colony stirred up trouble, and Virginia and the Dutch continued their disputes over boundaries. But, even so, except for a few arguments among the colonists, there was a feeling of peace.

The colony was growing fast. By now, the choice land along the Chesapeake Bay, the Patuxent River, the Potomac, the Choptank, and all other waterways deep enough to float a barge had been settled by wealthy landowners. Inland, most of the land had been divided into small farms belonging to men of modest purses and to indentured servants who had earned fifty acres, along with a horse, a plow, and their freedom.

Everybody grew tobacco. Manors on the water had their own shipping wharves. Bridle paths and Indian trails were widened into roads, and hogsheads of tobacco were rolled down them to the waiting ships.

One road led from the tobacco country to St. Mary's, where a man could buy and sell at market on Saturday, and on Sunday take his family to church. Another road, the busiest of all, led to Providence. On this road slow-moving farm wagons were often left behind by carriages full of ladies and gentlemen hurrying into town. Providence was the place to go for the latest news, the latest fashion, and the latest gossip. It was now the largest, busiest town in Maryland.

Cecil Calvert still knew Maryland only by hearsay. Sitting at his desk, far away in England, he studied the map of his colony, read letters from his son, and tried to picture his land in the New World. Those fine lines on the map were to him real rivers, full of fish; they were streams where boys waded, their breeches rolled up to the knees. Between rivers, trails crossed the country, through woods and out into sunlight again. Roads passed plantations with white manor houses set way back in shady groves of trees. It was the people who lived in the houses and worked in the fields that Cecil knew best. From

hundreds of letters over the years, from long talks with his own family, from snatches of conversations with ship captains and merchants, he learned to know the colonists, their hopes and fears.

Maryland was all that Cecil had planned, all that his father had dreamed. Cecil remembered hearing George Calvert say forty years before, "There should be a place where a man could live in peace, free to worship God as he pleased." Maryland was that place, praise be to God!

Lord Baltimore remembered clearly when the *Ark* and the *Dove* first sailed from Cowes. His brothers, Father White, Cornwallis, the Wintours were all young men then. Most of them were gone, George and Leonard both buried in the New World; friends left were getting old.

According to the report from the last Assembly, there were now twenty thousand Marylanders, children and grandchildren of the first settlers; also new families from Europe.

Once again, Cecil wished he could go to Maryland, as he had wished so many times.

His wish never came true. On November 30, 1675, Cecil Calvert, Second Lord Baltimore, died at the age of sixty-nine. His friends in England mourned for him. He had been a gentle man, wise and just, an Englishman of integrity and strong character. If there was one quality that shone above the others it was unselfishness. Cecil Calvert thought of his country, his colony, his family, never of himself.

To Marylanders, he was almost a legend, the Lord Proprietary who protected them from dangers and struggled to preserve their freedom for them. Although George Calvert was responsible for the idea of religious freedom, Cecil was the one who made the idea work.

With Cecil dead, the title Baron of Baltimore passed to his son, Charles Calvert, Maryland's Governor, who was now called Lord Baltimore. The words "Our Governor, Lord Baltimore," had quite a ring to them. If, by chance, anyone met the Governor on the courthouse steps, it was pleasant to greet him with, "Good day, Your Lordship."

His Lordship left his eight-year-old son, Little Cis, as Acting Governor, with counselors to speak for him, and sailed to England to settle his father's affairs. He stayed there no longer than necessary, for now that he was both Lord Proprietary and Governor, he had even more duties waiting for him at home.

Charles Calvert was not as wise as his father. Unlike his father, he wanted power for himself. With this in mind, he packed the Upper House of the Maryland Assembly with relatives and Catholic friends whose votes he could influence.

Before long, because of his highhanded ways, the Third Lord Baltimore found that he was not popular. England was also becoming unpopular in Maryland, for she was taking too much tobacco and collecting too many high taxes. Marylanders began to grumble.

In 1684, Charles Calvert again traveled to England. This time he left his second son, Benedict Leonard, five years old, in his place, again with counselors to guide the government. The much beloved Little Cis had died in 1681 at the age of fourteen.

While Charles was in England, William, Prince of Orange, and Mary, daughter of James II, came to the throne. At once, Lord Baltimore sent a messenger to Maryland with the news, ordering Marylanders to obey the new King and Queen. Unfortunately, the man died on the voyage, and by the time a second messenger had made the long, slow trip across the ocean, there had been an uprising in Maryland.

The earliest colonists had gotten along well with the Pascataway Indians, until that tribe moved away and the fierce northern Senecas came south. Soon, raids and scalpings spread fear all over Maryland. Rumors flew like wild geese. Some said ten thousand Senecas had gathered at the mouth of the Patuxent River. Others declared that the Maryland Catholics had invited the warriors to join the French colonists and help chase the Protestants out of Maryland. Whether or not ex-Governor Josiah Fendall, still eager to stir up trouble and seize control of the colony, started these rumors, no one was sure, but it was known that he was traveling around the province talking against Lord Baltimore.

One John Coode, a Protestant, having been appointed to the Lower House of the Assembly, listened to the rumors eagerly. He, too, was full of ambition for political power and was plotting to overthrow the government of the colony. Here was his chance to attack Lord Baltimore, under the pretext of protecting Maryland from the Indians, so he gathered a force of colonists and rushed out to meet the Senecas. But where were the Senecas? Not one could be found.

Another rumor said that the band of Indians had moved on to Mattaponi Fort. Many able-bodied men left their work to their wives, if they were fortunate enough to have them, and joined Coode's army, marching to St. Mary's City. There were no Indians there either.

Coode found the loyal supporters of Lord Baltimore gathered at Mattaponi Fort to make a last stand against his forces. However, with a thousand well-armed men, he was able to take over the government with little bloodshed. He removed all of Lord Baltimore's relatives and friends from the Upper House of the Assembly, and appointed his followers, all Protestants. Then he declared himself Governor.

Coode now realized that these highhanded actions had to be explained to the new King and Queen. He sent a message to Their Majesties, stating that Lord Baltimore was trying to keep Maryland from pledging allegiance to them. Coode and the Speaker of the Upper House of the Maryland Assembly were ordered to report to England. Lord Baltimore, still in London, was also given a hearing, but the Lords of the Privy Council in Parliament chose to believe Coode. In a Protestant government, which England had now, the word of another Protestant was more likely to be believed than that of a Catholic. So, King William and Queen Mary took Maryland away from Lord Baltimore and made it a royal colony.

This was a bitter blow to Charles. "Had I been in Maryland myself," he said ruefully to his wife, "this would never have happened."

"Had you been there, a wild Seneca Indian might have gotten your scalp," she replied. "Even if you are no longer Proprietary of Maryland, you are still Lord Baltimore."

"Thanks be to God for that," Charles answered, "and, as Lord Baltimore, I shall continue to receive the quit rents from the colony. With prices so high in England we will sorely need those monies."

Royal Governor Lionel Copley arrived at St. Mary's early in 1692, sent from England by the Royal Sovereigns. Coode turned the government of the colony over to him. Copley called the Assembly and established the Anglican Church as the official church of Maryland. This was the end of the idea of religious toleration upon which Maryland had been established.

12

An End and a Beginning

FOR TWENTY-FOUR YEARS, Maryland was ruled by royal governors—seven of them—some good, others not. They all had one thing in common, difficulty in collecting their salaries from the Maryland Assembly. The colonists realized that in order to retain their liberty, they had to control the spending of public monies, and they used this power to its fullest extent. During these twenty-four years, Charles Calvert, the Third Lord Baltimore, lived quietly in Kiplin, England, with his family.

His son, Benedict Leonard, married Lady Charlotte Lee, granddaughter of King Charles II. The marriage pleased Charles Calvert. But some years later, when Benedict Leonard became a Protestant, Charles was not at all pleased. Although he had learned tolerance in the cradle, he could not forgive his own son for leaving the Catholic Church.

He refused to give Benedict Leonard any more money. This was a blow to the young man for, by this time, he had seven children, all in expensive Protestant boarding schools. Luckily for Benedict, Protestant Queen Anne, who followed William and Mary as ruler of England, gave him a pension. This pension was kept up by George I when he came to the throne.

When Charles died on February 20, 1715, at the age of eighty-five, Benedict Leonard succeeded to the title. He might have made a good Proprietary. No one will ever know, for he died April 5, 1715, having been the Fourth Lord Baltimore for only six weeks.

Benedict's son, Charles, at sixteen years of age, became the Baron of Baltimore, the Fifth Lord Baltimore. His guardian immediately brought to the attention of King George I the fact that the new Lord Baltimore was a Protestant and therefore there was no longer any reason for not returning the colony to the Baltimores. The King agreed. The next month, Maryland was given to Charles, under the terms of the original charter granted eighty-three years earlier to George Calvert, his great-great-grandfather.

Charles, the Fifth Lord Baltimore, was proud of his title and his own importance. In 1729, it was "Enacted by the Right Honorable the Lord Proprietary . . . with the Advice and Consent of His Lordship's Governour, and the Upper and Lower Houses of Assembly" that a new town be built on the north side of the Patapsco River and called by the name of Baltimore Town. The first three streets were named Charles, Calvert, and Baltimore. Charles took no chances that anyone in the years to come would forget who he was.

Three years later, Charles and his lady left London and the fashionable life of the English Court to pay a visit to his colony. They landed at Providence, the new capital, recently renamed Annapolis, in honor of Queen Anne. Charles brought along a handsome portrait of himself, painted especially for the colony, and presented it to his people on his arrival. They accepted the painting graciously and proudly hung it in the Assembly Hall on Duke of Gloucester Street in Annapolis.

Like the paintings of his father, grandfather, great-grandfather, and great-great-grandfather, it was a large, full-length portrait. In it, Charles wore a white, military wig, close fitting and tied in back. He held his head high and seemed to be looking down his long, straight nose. His blue coat had brass buttons down the front, and wide cuffs, lined in pale blue satin. His waistcoat was brocaded cloth of gold. On his chest shone a burnished breastplate. The provincial seal of Maryland stood at his right hand, with a Maryland Indian, almost lost in the shadows beyond. Off to the left, the *Ark* and the *Dove* sailed across a painted sea. The artist, determined not to leave out anything, included the flag of the Calvert family and a quiver of arrows in the foreground.

Lord and Lady Baltimore felt that they would impress their colony with their magnificent clothes and courtly polish. However, to their surprise, they found almost as glittering a social life as they had left in England. There were many balls, dinners, and musicales, but the fanciest one of all was a ball in honor of Lady Baltimore's birthday.

The Maryland Gazette for February 9, 1733, gave this account:

> "Last Tuesday being the Birth-Day of the Right Honorable the Lady Baltimore, the same was observed here, with all Demonstrations of Joy. The Fort Guns were fired at One of the Clock, which was handsomely returned by the Man of War, and other ships lying here. In the Evening His Lordship gave the Ladies a Ball, which concluded suitable to the happy Occasion. . . ."

The Annapolis Ballroom on King George Street was lighted with hundreds of wax tapers. Lady Baltimore was the center of attention in her gold brocade skirt, overlaid with lace. Her bodice was of rose velvet, with lacy sleeves caught up with velvet bows to match. Her fan, from the Far East, was of exquisitely carved ivory.

His Lordship, in rose velvet longcoat handsomely embroidered in gold was a match for his lady. The delicate lace at his cuffs and neck was of the finest Flemish design. As the noble pair led the figures of the minuet, his handsomely turned legs were the envy of the gallants.

While the dancers went through the intricate figures to the lilting music of harpsichord, violins, and flutes, Lord Baltimore thought to himself that it was a finer thing to be the only lord in Maryland than one of many at the English Court.

Being the Lord Proprietary and Governor was not all pleasure, as Charles was soon to find out. It would take more than a portrait and fine clothes to impress the Assembly. When he tried to tell the men to pass new tax laws which would give him more money, the Lower House flatly refused. Nevertheless, the Proprietary saw to it that every penny due him in rents and taxes was collected, a sum amounting to about ten thousand pounds sterling or about fifty thousand dollars a year.

After a six months' visit, Lord and Lady Baltimore went back to England. By this time everyone was glad to see them go! Not only had Charles offended the members of the Assembly with his greedy demands, but he had also surrendered thousands of acres of valuable Maryland land to Pennsylvania in the north and to Virginia in the south. Cecil and Charles had been able to hold these lands

in their times, but this Fifth Lord Baltimore handed them over without a struggle.

Charles died April 24, 1751, without ever returning to Maryland. He was a good-natured, vain, weak man who understood little of the problems of his colony.

His son Frederick, who became Sixth Lord Baltimore, was twenty years old when his father died. For one year, while he was still a minor, his guardians were John Sharpe, Esq., a lawyer; and the Right Honorable Arthur Onslow, Speaker of the House of Commons. These important gentlemen needed more than one year to make a man of Frederick, for he was weak and no credit to his famous name.

In 1753 Lord Baltimore married Lady Diana Egerton. After three years of marriage they separated by mutual agreement. This unhappy lady was doubly unfortunate; an invalid, with no children. She had been thrown from a carriage in an accident while out driving with her husband and suffered a back injury from which she never recovered. However, until the time of her death, in 1758, she was fond of Lord Baltimore, in spite of his weakness, greed, and vanity.

Although Frederick traveled all over Europe, going as far as Constantinople, he never bothered to visit Maryland. He cared nothing for his colony; only the money he got from it. By this time he was receiving $60,000.00 a year from taxes and rents, enough to let him travel in luxury. Frederick wrote a book about his travels, and several volumes of verse, which he had published at his own expense. He was very proud of these writings, an opinion which the critics did not share.

Frederick ruined his reputation by his wild and extravagant manner of living. London was buzzing with stories about his Lordship, and soon the gossip crossed the Atlantic to his colony of Maryland. Not only was Frederick talked about at parties, taverns, and supper tables, but even by the freemen of the Maryland Assembly.

One member spoke for all when he said, "Taxes, taxes, taxes, to King George the Third and to Lord Baltimore. That's all they want of the colony; stamp taxes, tea taxes, and on top of that our Assembly seems to be financing Frederick Calvert's wicked ways."

They all nodded in agreement.

The Assembly did not have to bear this burden too long, for in 1771, Frederick Calvert, Baron of Baltimore, the Sixth and last Lord Baltimore, died at the age of forty, and the title died with him.

Frederick left no legitimate children, but he willed Maryland to his illegitimate son, Henry Harford. Maryland was not pleased. However, through the influence of the Governor, Robert Eden, husband of Frederick's younger sister, the Assembly honored Frederick's claim and accepted Henry Harford as the Proprietary. For the next five years, Maryland suffered greatly. Taxes increased; land, already worn out from raising too much tobacco, became poorer still; money, needed to build schools and roads, ended up in the King's purse or in Henry Harford's pocket.

At last, Maryland rebelled. The Maryland colony, founded by George Calvert, the First Lord Baltimore, and established by Cecil Calvert, the Second Lord Baltimore, was now strong and ready for freedom. The Assembly bought Harford's claim to the colony for a generous sum of money. The Maryland Convention to the Continental Congress decided that Governor Eden's usefulness was ended and courteously informed him that he was at liberty to leave. This he did, promptly, returning to England by the first ship.

For two years, Maryland delegates to the Continental Congress had been working on laws for their own colony, as well as helping Virginia, Plymouth, and the other colonies unite against England. On July 3, 1776, the delegates, assembled in the Maryland Convention, declared the colony to be independent of England, independent of the Proprietary. The very next day, July 4, 1776, the Declaration of Independence of the United States of America was proclaimed by the Continental Congress.

Bibliography

Agle, Nan Hayden. *Princess Mary of Maryland.* New York: Charles Scribner's Sons, 1956.

Andrews, Matthew Page. *The Founding of Maryland.* Baltimore: The Williams & Wilkins Co., 1933.

————. *The History of Maryland; Province and State.* New York: Doubleday & Company, Inc., 1929.

Bacon, Frances A., and Foster, James W. *Living in Colonial Maryland.* Baltimore: The Enoch Pratt Free Library.

Bibbins, Mrs. Arthur Barneveld. *The Beginnings of Maryland.* Baltimore: Remington, 1934.

Brown, William Hand. *George Calvert and Cecilius Calvert.* New York: Dodd, Mead & Co., 1890.

Browne, William Hand (ed.). "Proccedings and Acts of the General Assembly of Maryland." Baltimore: Maryland Historical Society, 1883.

Bump Papers. In Manuscript. Courtesy of the Maryland Historical Society.

Forman, Henry Chandler. *Jamestown and St. Mary's.* Baltimore: The Johns Hopkins Press, 1938.

Foster, James W. "George Calvert: His Yorkshire Boyhood," *Maryland Historical Magazine*, Vol. 55, No. 4 (December, 1960).

————, and Manakee, Beta K. *The Lords Baltimore*. Pamphlet. Baltimore: Enoch Pratt Free Library, 1942.

Green, Elmer. *The Making of Maryland*. Baltimore: E. & M. Green, 1934.

Hall, Clayton Colman. *The Lords Baltimore and the Maryland Palatinate*. Baltimore: John Murphy Company, 1902.

Hawks, Francis F. *A Relation of Maryland*. New York: Joseph Sabin, 1865.

Hunter, Wilbur Harvey, Jr. "The Portrait of Charles Calvert, Fifth Lord Baltimore." *The Peale Museum Historical Series*, Publication No. 12, Baltimore, 1957.

Inglis, R. B., Stauffer, D. A., and Larsen, C. E. *Adventures in English Literature*. New York: Harcourt, Brace & Co., 1952.

Ives, J. Moss. *The Ark and the Dove*. New York: Longmans, Green & Co., Inc., 1936.

Kaessman, Beta, Manakee, H. R., and Wheeler, J. L. *My Maryland*. Boston: Ginn & Company, 1934.

Kingsley, Charles. *Westward Ho!* New York: Charles Scribner's Sons, 1920.

Lunt, W. E. *History of England*. New York: Harper & Brothers, 1956.

McElwee, William. *Wisest Fool in Christendom*. London: Faber & Faber Ltd., 1958.

Manakee, Harold R. *Indians of Early Maryland*. Baltimore: Maryland Historical Society, 1959.

Neill, Edward D. *Terra Mariae, or Threads of Maryland Colonial History*. Philadelphia: J. B. Lippincott Co., 1867.

Passano, L. Magruder. *Maryland; Stories of Her People and Her History*. Baltimore: The Williams & Wilkins Co., 1924.

Quennell, Marjorie, and Quennell, C. H. B. *A History of Everyday Things in England,* Part 2. New York: Charles Scribner's Sons, 1935.

Russell, William T. *Maryland: The Land of Sanctuary*. Baltimore: J. H. Furst Company, 1908.

Scharf, J. Thomas. *History of Maryland,* Vol. I. Baltimore: John B. Piet, 1879.

Steiner, Bernard C. *Beginnings of Maryland*. Baltimore: The Johns Hopkins Press, 1903.

Streeter, Sebastian F. "Papers Relating to the Early History of Maryland." Baltimore: Maryland Historical Society, January, 1876.

Thomas, James Walter. *Chronicles of Colonial Maryland*. Cumberland, Maryland: Eddy Press, 1913.

Whitbourne, Richard. *Westward Hoe for Avalon, in the New-Found-Land*. London: S. Lowe Son and Marston, 1870.

The World Book Encyclopedia. Chicago: Field Enterprises Educational Corporation, 1950.

ABOUT THE AUTHORS

Nan Hayden Agle and Frances Atchinson Bacon became friends when Mrs. Agle was the favorite teacher of Mrs. Bacon's daughter. Both writers live in Baltimore, and have established reputations as authors of children's books.

Mrs. Agle grew up in Maryland. She attended Goucher College and the Maryland Institute. An artist in her own right, she has taught painting at the Baltimore Friends School, and now teaches children's classes at the Baltimore Museum of Art.

Mrs. Bacon was born and brought up in Michigan. After studying at the Carnegie Library School, she became a children's librarian. After moving to Maryland, she continued her work with children at the Enoch Pratt Free Library. Instrumental in founding the School of the Chimes, Inc., a nonprofit day school for retarded children, Mrs. Bacon is active on its Board of Directors.

Date L